MW01617390

SCOTT FORESMAN

SOCIAL STUDIES

NEW MEXICO

PEARSON

Scott
Foresman

Editorial Offices: Glenview, Illinois • Parsippany, New Jersey • New York, New York
Sales Offices: Parsippany, New Jersey • Duluth, Georgia • Glenview, Illinois •
Coppell, Texas • Ontario, California • Mesa, Arizona

www.sfsocialstudies.com

TEACHER REVIEWERS

Julia M. Chaney
Reading Specialist
Hobbs Municipal School District
Hobbs, New Mexico

Cheryl Cunningham
Cameo Elementary School
Clovis, New Mexico

ISBN: 0-328-09139-1

3 4 5 6 7 8 9 10 V034 12 11 10 09 08 07 06 05

Contents

New Mexico

Chapter 1

The Geography of New Mexico   **5**

"I think New Mexico was the greatest experience from the outside world that I have ever had. It certainly changed me for ever."

— D. H. Lawrence, from his essay "New Mexico" (1928)

Chapter 2

The History of New Mexico   **45**

Contents

New Mexico

John Sloan spent many summers in Santa Fe. He often painted outdoor scenes, such as *Chama Running Red.*

"**I think New Mexico was the greatest experience from the outside world that I have ever had. It certainly changed me for ever.**"

—D. H. Lawrence, from his essay "New Mexico" (1928)

Welcome to New Mexico

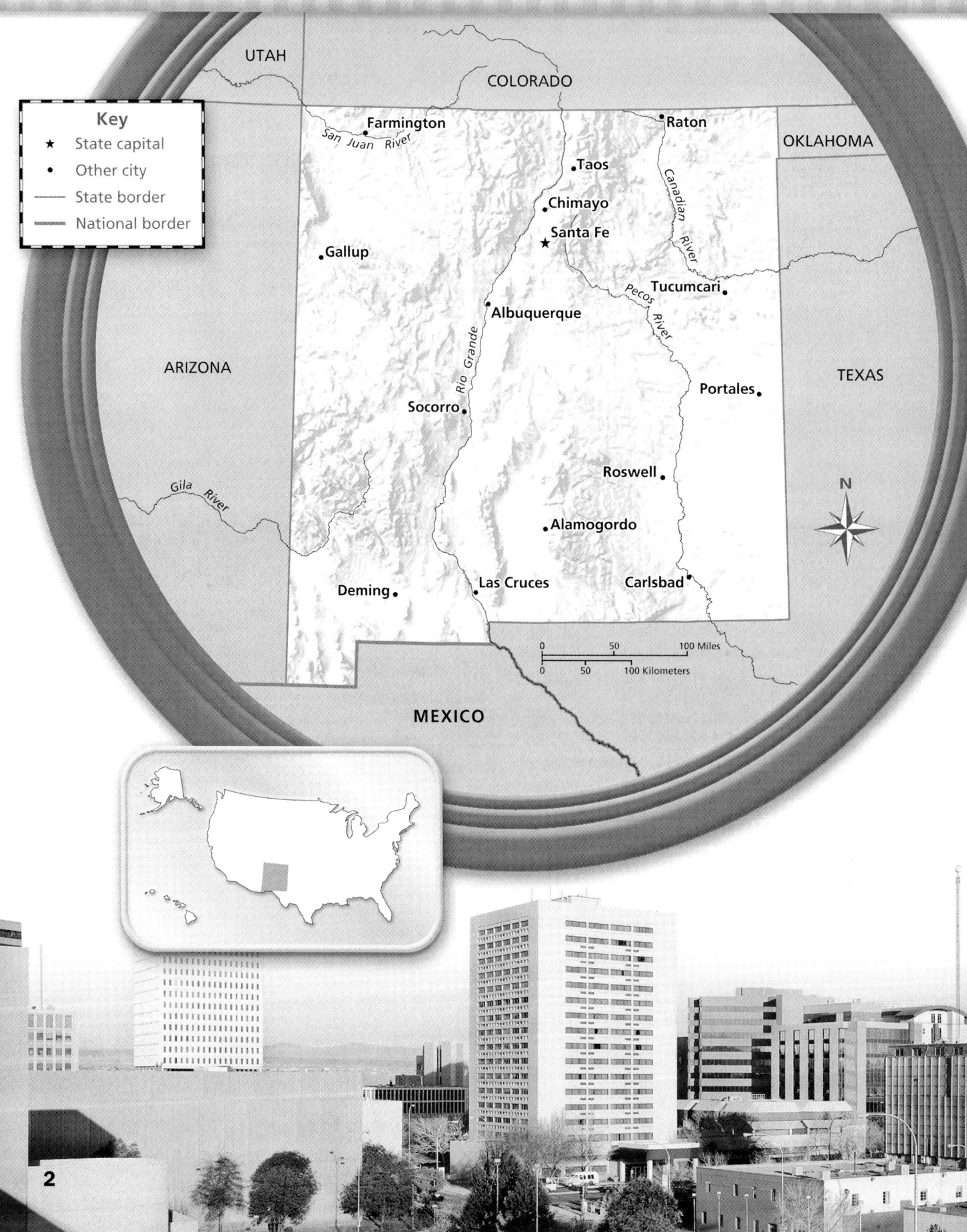

Key
★ State capital
● Other city
— State border
— National border

UTAH
COLORADO
Farmington
San Juan River
Raton
OKLAHOMA
Taos
Chimayo
Santa Fe
Canadian River
Gallup
Tucumcari
Albuquerque
Pecos River
ARIZONA
TEXAS
Portales
Socorro
Roswell
Gila River
Alamogordo
N
Deming
Las Cruces
Carlsbad

0   50   100 Miles
0   50   100 Kilometers

MEXICO

▶ Chimayo is home to many weavers who make colorful blankets, rugs, and clothing.

▶ Ship Rock is a huge volcanic rock that early settlers thought resembled a sailing ship. Located near Farmington, it can be seen from great distances.

▶ The brown and white roadrunner is New Mexico's state bird. It is usually seen running along the ground because it is clumsy when it flies.

▶ New Mexico's snow-covered mountains are popular with skiers.

▶ This special equipment, located in Albuquerque, allows scientists to study very small bits of matter.

▶ Albuquerque is New Mexico's largest city and home to the University of New Mexico, the Indian Pueblo Cultural Center, and the National Hispanic Cultural Center.

Reading Social Studies

Summarize

A summary is a short statement that describes a longer piece of text. A good summary presents all the important information briefly and clearly.

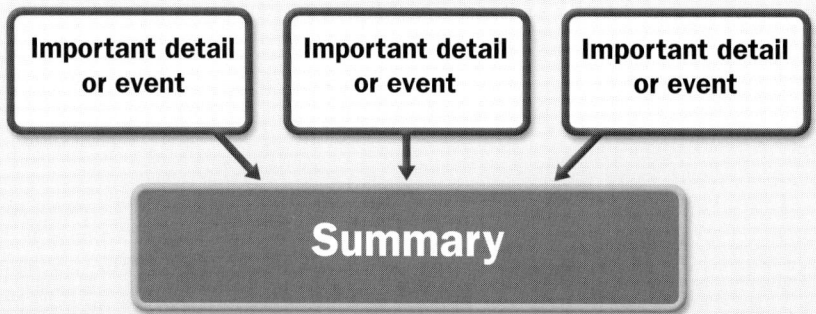

- A summary should include only the main facts or information from the text.
- Learning to summarize can help you remember the most important parts of the material you read.

New Mexico: The Land of Enchantment

New Mexico is a varied land of great beauty. You can see snow-covered mountains, sparkling rivers, and grassy plains throughout our state. It is known as the Land of Enchantment.

New Mexico has also been known as the Sunshine State. Three of every four days are sunny. The climate is generally warm and dry.

New Mexico's beauty and climate have drawn many different groups of people to our state. Festivals feature the music, foods, crafts, and other traditions of New Mexico's diverse people.

Use the reading strategy of summarizing to answer these questions.

1. What three main ideas are contained in the passage above?

2. List details that support the main ideas.

3. Rewrite your main ideas and supporting details to create a short, clear summary of the passage.

The Geography of New Mexico

CHAPTER 1

Lesson 1

Wheeler Peak

Located in the Rocky Mountains, Wheeler Peak is the highest point in New Mexico.

Lesson 2

Gila National Forest

After a long absence, wolves have been brought back to New Mexico to live in Gila National Forest.

Lesson 3

Eddy County

Oil and gas wells dot Eddy County and other areas.

Lesson 4

Las Cruces

Las Cruces is an important agricultural center.

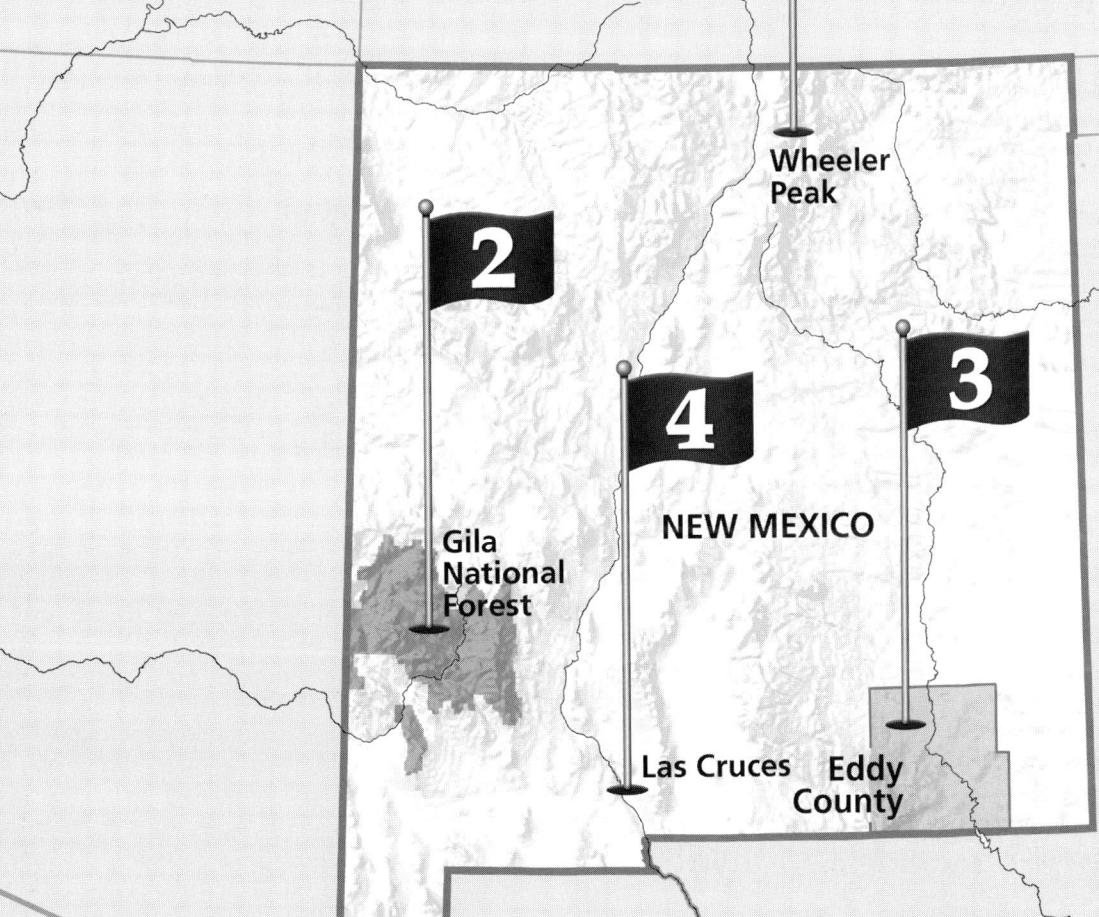

Wheeler Peak

Gila National Forest

NEW MEXICO

Las Cruces   Eddy County

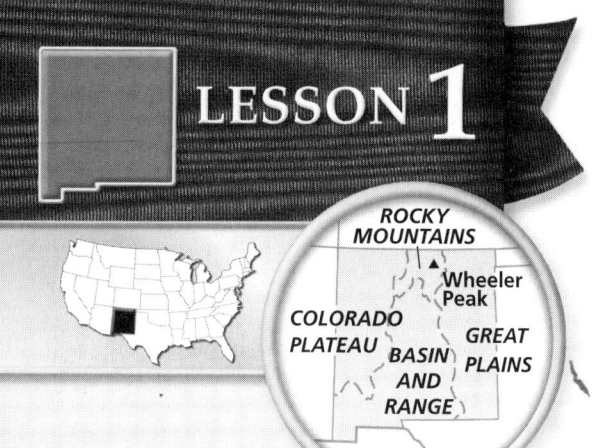

ROCKY
MOUNTAINS

Wheeler
Peak

COLORADO
PLATEAU

GREAT
PLAINS

BASIN
AND
RANGE

PREVIEW

Focus on the Main Idea
New Mexico's regions feature many different kinds of landforms.

PLACES
Great Plains region
Rocky Mountains region
Colorado Plateau region
Basin and Range region
Wheeler Peak
Rio Grande

PEOPLE
Jim White
Georgia O'Keeffe

VOCABULARY
mesa
crater
natural gas
basin
tributary

TERM
cinder cone

▶ Visitors who fly to New Mexico can view snowcapped mountains in the north.

A Varied Land

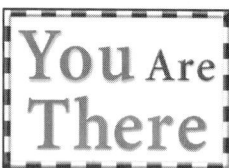
You Are There

You and your family are returning home after visiting your grandparents. You have spent most of the flight looking out the airplane window at the amazing shapes and patterns on the land below.

As the airplane flies toward Albuquerque, you see sunlight sparkle on the snowcapped peaks to the north. In another direction you can see wide, grassy plains. The Rio Grande looks like a shiny silver ribbon stretching southward. Mountain ranges spread across the land.

This view from above shows you just how beautiful your state is. Now you understand why New Mexico is called the Land of Enchantment!

Summarize As you read, look for details that will help you summarize New Mexico's physical features and regions.

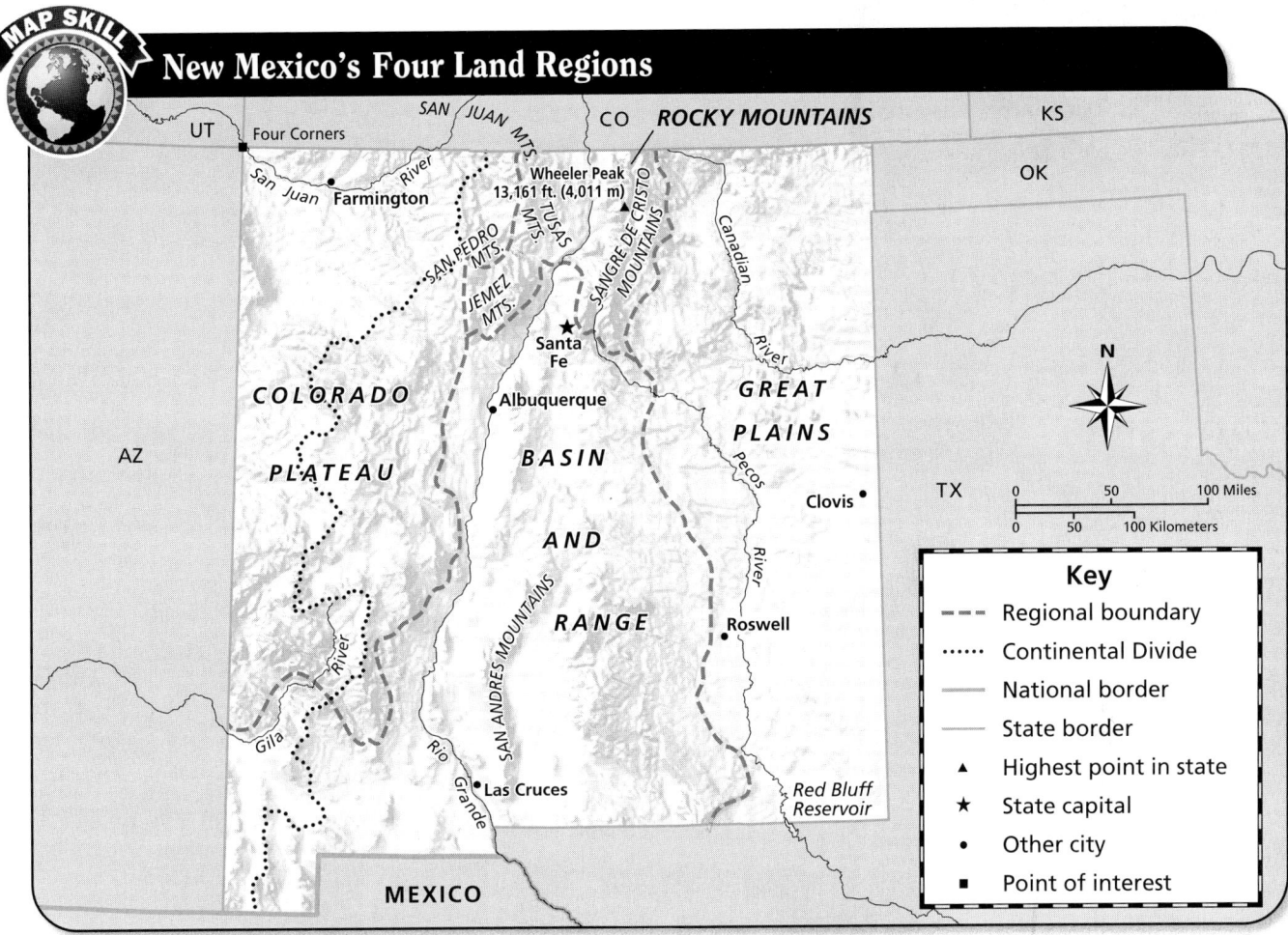

▶ Various physical features are found in New Mexico's four land regions.

MAP SKILL Understand Borders *Which three states border New Mexico at the Four Corners?*

Discover New Mexico

New Mexico's land is as varied, or different, as it is large. New Mexico is the fifth-largest state in the United States. It is made up of four provinces, or regions. A region is an area in which places share similar characteristics. The Great Plains region features broad grasslands. The Rocky Mountains region is known for its rugged mountains. The Colorado Plateau region has plateaus, canyons, and river valleys. The Basin and Range region features the Rio Grande valley, mountains, and deserts. The beauty and variety of these regions have led people to call New Mexico the Land of Enchantment.

In northwestern New Mexico, there is a monument called the Four Corners. It marks the only place in the United States where the borders of four states meet.

New Mexico is located in the Southwest region of the United States. This region is generally sunny and warm with mountains, canyons, and deserts. Arizona, Texas, and Oklahoma border our state and are also located in the Southwest region. Utah and Colorado also border New Mexico. Part of New Mexico's southern border is a national border that is shared with the country of Mexico.

REVIEW How can New Mexico's land features be described? ⟳ **Summarize**

7

The Great Plains Region

The Great Plains region is part of a high plain that extends across the central United States. As you can see on the map below, the Great Plains region covers the eastern third of New Mexico. The land here supports farming, ranching, and mining.

Two of New Mexico's major rivers stretch across the Great Plains region like long fingers. The Pecos River begins high in the Rocky Mountains region, northeast of the city of Santa Fe. It flows south across the plains for hundreds of miles until it reaches Texas. The Canadian River also flows from the Rocky Mountains region. It crosses the northern part of the Great Plains region and then turns east into Texas.

If you were looking at this region from above, you would notice changes in its landscape. Deep valleys and mesas mark the land north of the Canadian River. A **mesa** is a small, high plateau with steep sides and a flat top.

Have you ever seen a high mountain? Capulin Mountain rises more than 1,200 feet from the plains around it. This is almost as tall as the Empire State Building in New York City. Capulin Mountain is actually a cinder cone. A **cinder cone** is a type of volcano made of loose material such as volcanic rocks and ash. Like the rest of the state's many volcanoes, Capulin Mountain stopped erupting thousands of years ago. If you visit there, you can look into its crater. A **crater** is a bowl-shaped hole around the opening of a volcano. You can even walk along a trail to the bottom of the crater and explore more of the volcano.

South of Capulin Mountain are wide grasslands. Early explorers reported that the grass stood higher than the backs of their horses. Today people can see natural grasses at Kiowa (KY uh wuh) National Grassland. Today farms and ranches dot the land.

▶ **This picture shows Kiowa National Grassland. Buffalo and the livestock brought by settlers grazed on grasslands such as this.**

South of the Canadian River lies the Llano Estacado (YA noh es tah KAH doh), or Staked Plains. This high plain is extremely flat. One early explorer who traveled there wrote,

"... [T]here is nowhere a stone, a hill, a tree, or a bush, or anything of the sort."

However, the land is good for ranching and farming.

Farther south are major deposits of oil and natural gas. **Natural gas** is a gas that forms underground. Homes and industries use natural gas as a fuel for heat and power.

In addition to valuable resources, the Great Plains region features Red Bluff Lake, the lowest point in New Mexico. This lake is located south of Carlsbad. Its elevation is about one-half mile above sea level.

Another remarkable feature near Carlsbad is Carlsbad Caverns National Park. A cavern is a large, deep cave. **Jim White,** a New Mexico cowhand, explored this natural wonder in the early

► **This room in Carlsbad Caverns is called the King's Palace. Another room in the cave is so large that six football fields could fit inside it.**

1900s. Since then, more than 100 miles of underground rooms and passages have been discovered. Thousands of bats live in the caverns and fly out each evening in the spring and summer months to feed. This amazing sight and the unusual caverns attract many tourists each year. Next you will learn about the Rocky Mountains region, which also attracts many visitors to the state.

REVIEW What are the main features of the Great Plains region? ⊙ **Summarize**

9

▶ Wheeler Peak's elevation is 13,161 feet. That is almost two and one-half miles above sea level.

The Rocky Mountains Region

The Rocky Mountains region is the smallest of our state's four regions. It is located in the center of northern New Mexico. This region extends south from the Colorado border and ends near Santa Fe.

The region is named for the Rocky Mountains. This long chain of mountains stretches north to south through western North America from Alaska to New Mexico.

The land in this region reaches high elevations. Forests of pine, fir, and aspen trees cover the mountainsides. However, on land near the mountaintops only a few small plants are able to survive the cold.

New Mexico's highest point, **Wheeler Peak,** is located in the Sangre de Cristo (SANG gray day KRIS toh) Mountains. This

mountain range is part of the Rocky Mountains and lies northeast of Santa Fe. Several other high mountains dot the region, including Truchas Peak.

A gorge is a deep, narrow valley. The Rio Grande Gorge, about 150 miles long, slices the land between the Sangre de Cristo Mountains to the east and the San Juan (san WAHN) and Tusas Mountains to the west. The state's longest river, the **Rio Grande,** flows along the bottom of the gorge.

New Mexico author Tony Hillerman wrote about the remarkable Rio Grande:

". . . [I]ts nineteen-hundred-mile journey to the Gulf of Mexico makes it second only to the Missouri-Mississippi in length among the continent's rivers."

ROCKY MOUNTAINS
▲ Wheeler Peak
Taos
▲ Truchas Peak
Rio Chama
Rio Grande
Pecos River
N

▶ **The Rio Grande flows through the Rocky Mountains region and continues south across the entire state.**

You might think that the Rio Grande's flowing water carved this gorge. However, forces deep inside Earth long ago caused the surface, or crust, of Earth to move and form cracks. The crust is the solid outside part of Earth. These same forces also created volcanoes in this area.

Because of these events, much of the rock in this region comes from deep inside Earth. Many scientists believe that the rock is millions of years old. In fact, astronauts have trained in this area to learn how to explore areas on the moon.

In addition to shaping the land, rivers here provide recreation for New Mexicans and visitors. People use both the Rio Grande and the Rio Chama for fishing and boating. The Rio Chama's canyon is not

as long as the Rio Grande Gorge, but it runs even deeper.

The Rio Chama area is also well known for another reason. The famous artist **Georgia O'Keeffe** lived in this area for almost forty years. Her paintings of the landscape helped make people more aware of New Mexico's great beauty.

South of Taos, the Rio Grande Gorge gradually widens into a larger valley where farming takes place. To the east, the Pecos River begins its journey south into the Great Plains region. Next you will learn about the Colorado Plateau region, which lies to the west.

REVIEW Why is this area called the Rocky Mountains region? 🔄 **Summarize**

Acoma Pueblo sits more than 350 feet high atop Acoma Rock, one of this region's mesas. It is one of the oldest settlements in the United States.

Ship Rock ■
Farmington •   San Juan R.

N

• Gallup   *COLORADO
               PLATEAU*
El Morro   ■ • Acoma Pueblo
National
Monument

Gila River

The Colorado Plateau Region

The Colorado Plateau region is a large plateau that covers parts of New Mexico, Colorado, Arizona, and Utah. This plateau covers much of western New Mexico. This part of New Mexico is called the Colorado Plateau region. You can see it on the map on this page. The Continental Divide crosses the region from north to south.

Features such as canyons, mesas, and rocky plateaus are found here. Some of these features were formed from erosion by wind and water. Other features came from the eruptions of ancient volcanoes.

Ship Rock, the remains of an ancient volcano, is one of the region's major features. Ship Rock is special to the Diné (dee NAY), or Navajo. They call it "winged rock." It rises more than 1,400 feet from the surrounding land. You will read more about Ship Rock on page 16.

Ship Rock is located in the San Juan Basin, southwest of the town of Shiprock. A **basin** is a bowl-shaped area of land surrounded by higher land. Within this basin, the San Juan River crosses the state's northwest corner.

The San Juan Basin contains important natural resources. The area produces oil, coal, and uranium. Uranium is a very heavy, white metal. It is used in producing nuclear energy. In addition, the rich soil of the San Juan River valley supports farming.

In the central part of the region, several small mountain ranges extend across the plateau. The Zuni Mountains are located southeast of Gallup. At their southern edge is the El Malpais (el mahl pah EES) National Monument. El Malpais means "The Badlands." There you can see an oddly twisted landscape with tunnels and caves. This strange-looking land was formed by lava flowing from erupting volcanoes. As the hot lava cooled, it hardened into unusual shapes.

West of El Malpais is the bluff, or high cliff, of El Morro National Monument. This bluff is also called "Inscription Rock." Early explorers often carved pictures and writings in the stone as they rested in its shade.

To the south, the San Francisco Mountains lie near the state's western border. The Gila (HEE luh) River and its tributaries flow through these mountains. A **tributary** is a stream or river that flows into a larger river.

Next you will read about the Basin and Range region. Our state's longest river flows through that region.

REVIEW Describe features in the Colorado Plateau region. ⟳ **Summarize**

▶ **El Morro was a landmark for early travelers.**

The Basin and Range Region

The Basin and Range region extends through the center of New Mexico to the state's "boot heel" in the southwest. This is a small strip of land shaped like the heel of a boot. The Basin and Range region is the largest of New Mexico's four regions. The Continental Divide enters this region from the Colorado Plateau region and continues across the state's southern border into Mexico.

Many small mountain ranges are located here. Broad, dry basins separate them. These basins include the Rio Grande valley and the Tularosa (too luh ROH suh) valley.

The Rio Grande flows south from the Rocky Mountains region. It travels though the Basin and Range region on its way to the Gulf of Mexico. Much of the region's farming takes place near its banks. New

▶ The Bosque del Apache National Wildlife Refuge provides a winter home for thousands of birds each year.

Mexico's largest city, Albuquerque, and the state capital, Santa Fe, are also located near this river.

East of the Rio Grande valley lies the desert area of the Tularosa valley. Nearby is another desert area, the Jornada del Muerto (hor NAH dah del MWAIR toh), which means "Journey of the Dead" in Spanish.

▶ Most of New Mexico's people and much of its agriculture can be found in the Rio Grande valley.

N

Santa Fe
Albuquerque
Rio Grande
BASIN AND RANGE
Alamogordo
Las Cruces

Few people live in these desert areas. Some desert land is used by the military for research. There is a huge radio telescope in a desert area called the Plains of San Agustin. Scientists use this telescope to learn about objects in space. A smaller area of land is reserved for wildlife. It is the San Andres National Wildlife Refuge near Las Cruces. Desert bighorn sheep, many kinds of birds, and other animals live there.

The valley of the Rio Grande provides land that is good for ranching. The land is also rich in copper and other minerals. Mining is especially important in the southwestern part of our state. Later you will read about New Mexico's climate, plants, and animals.

REVIEW Summarize the natural resources of the Basin and Range region.
⏲ **Summarize**

▶ **White Sands National Monument has white sand dunes made of a mineral called gypsum.**

Summarize the Lesson

- New Mexico is part of the Southwest region of the United States.

- The state's four provinces, or regions, are the Great Plains region, the Rocky Mountains region, the Colorado Plateau region, and the Basin and Range region.

- Each region has physical features that make it unique.

LESSON 1   REVIEW

Check Facts and Main Ideas

1. ⏲ **Summarize** Complete the chart on a separate sheet of paper. Write a summary of the details shown below.

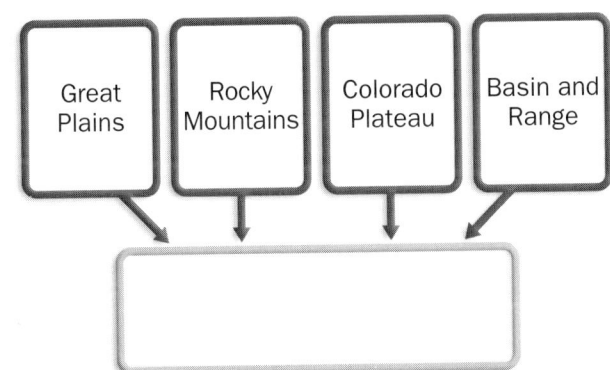

| Great Plains | Rocky Mountains | Colorado Plateau | Basin and Range |

2. Describe the Great Plains region.
3. Describe the Rocky Mountains region.
4. Describe the Colorado Plateau region.
5. **Critical Thinking:** *Express Opinions* Describe the features of the Basin and Range region that you think would attract people to live there.

Link to 🔗 Science

Research Landforms Choose a landform such as a **mesa** or a **basin,** or a specific place in your area. Research whether it was formed by volcanic eruption, by shifts in Earth's crust, or by water or wind erosion. Report your findings to the class.

HERE AND THERE

Hawaii and New Mexico

Volcanoes

Both New Mexico and Hawaii are part of the United States, but they differ greatly. New Mexico is on the North American continent. Hawaii is made up of several islands in the Pacific Ocean. However, volcanoes are important to each state's geography.

Hawaii is the only state formed by volcanoes. For example, today lava flows from Kilauea (KEE LOO AY ah), a volcano on Hawaii. As the lava flows into the Pacific Ocean, it cools and hardens to form new land.

New Mexico has hundreds of volcanoes. Most have not erupted for thousands of years. Lava from their early eruptions formed much of New Mexico's landscape.

▶ In the northeastern part of our state, Capulin Mountain is a volcano that has changed very little over time.

▶ Kilauea is the world's most active volcano. It has been slowly erupting for more than 20 years. It is one of five volcanoes on the island of Hawaii.

Ship Rock, in northwestern New Mexico, was formed from lava that hardened inside a very old volcano. Today the volcano is gone, and only the rock remains.

16

Jim White

1882–1946

Jim White was working as a cowhand in 1898 when he saw a cloud coming from the ground. He thought it was the eruption of a volcano. When he got closer, White saw that thousands of bats were flying out of a hole in the ground. Later White returned to the hole and looked down into it. He could not see to the bottom, but he knew that it had to be a huge cave in order to hold that many bats.

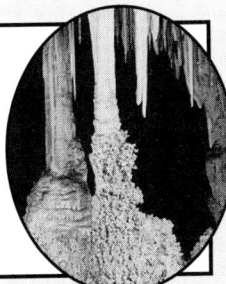

BIOFACT

White tied long pieces of string to formations such as these as he explored so that he would not become lost.

A few days later using a rope ladder and a lantern, White climbed down into the hole. The huge cavern he saw amazed him.

"The beauty, the weirdness, the grandeur . . . absolved [freed] my mind of all thought of a world above—I forgot time, place, and distance."

Jim White's natural curiosity led him to explore what came to be called Carlsbad Caverns. In 1898, when he was sixteen years old, he signed his name in the cave. For many years White talked about the caverns and guided people inside. The photo at the right shows White at the cave opening. Today we know this underground wonder as the main feature of Carlsbad Caverns National Park.

Learn from Biographies

Why do you think Jim White kept telling people about the caverns for many years?

OLD BUCKET AT TOP OF SHAFT THAT TOOK THE FIRST TOURISTS INTO CARLSBAD CAVERNS

Students can research the lives of significant people by clicking on *Meet the People* at **www.sfsocialstudies.com**.

17

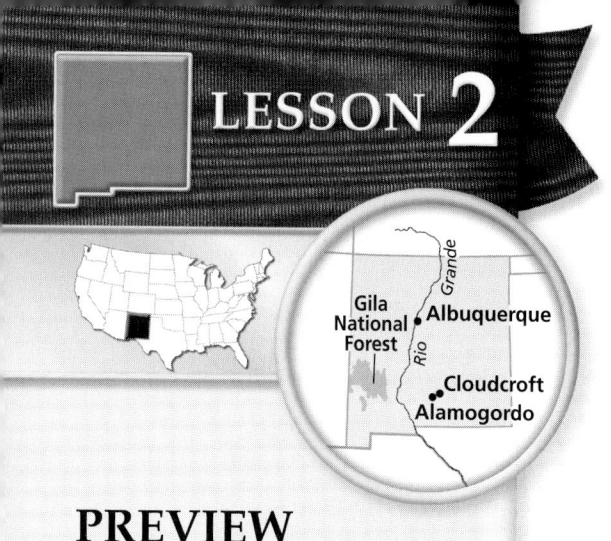

Gila
National
Forest

Rio Grande

Albuquerque

Cloudcroft
Alamogordo

Climate, Plants, and Animals

PREVIEW

Focus on the Main Idea
New Mexico's geography affects climate, settlement, and plants and animals.

PLACES
Cloudcroft
Albuquerque
Alamogordo
Rio Grande valley
Gila National Forest

VOCABULARY
revolve
rotate
hemisphere
environment
ecosystem
predator

▶ Elk live in New Mexico's mountains.

You Are There

Your family is camping tonight at Manzano Mountains State Park, southeast of Albuquerque. You saw an elk among nearby trees when you arrived. Many other animals and plants are quite different from the ones you saw when you were camping a couple of days ago. Then you were camped at Valley of Fires Recreation Area in the Tularosa valley.

Today you saw a variety of trees, including alligator junipers. The park ranger said that the alligator juniper got its name because its bark looks like an alligator's skin!

As you sit around the campfire, you feel cold. Your mother tells you that temperatures are usually cooler at higher elevations. Being in the mountains also makes you feel closer to the moon and the millions of sparkling stars.

Main Idea and Details As you read, look for details about how the relationship between Earth and the sun produces day and night, the seasons, and variations in climate.

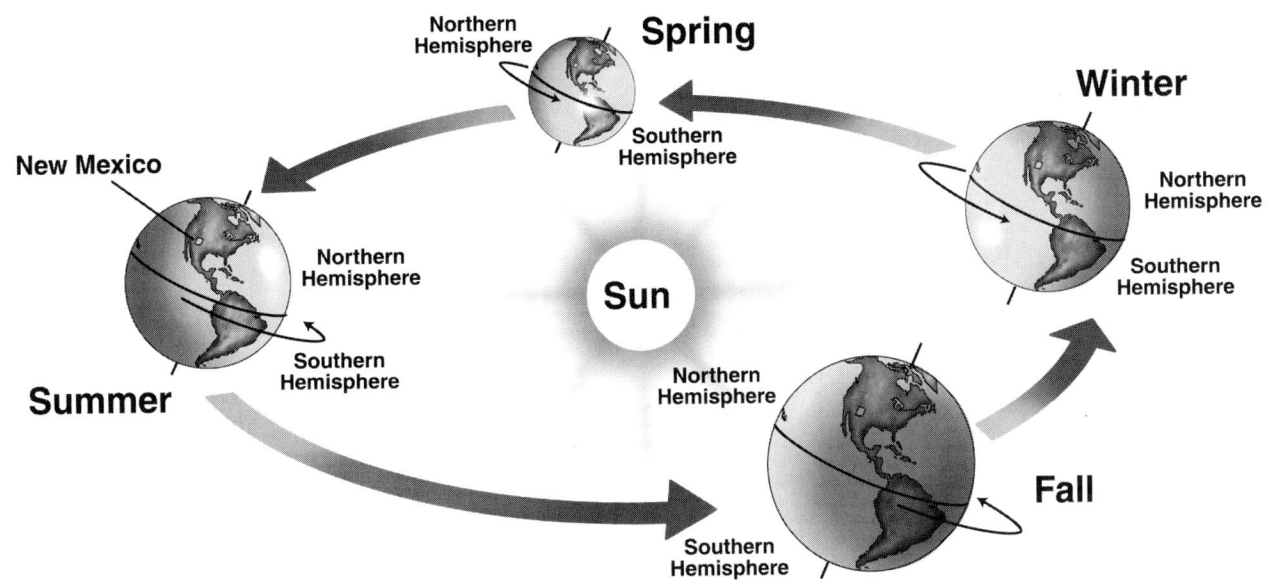

Spring

Winter

Summer

Fall

Northern Hemisphere
Southern Hemisphere
New Mexico
Northern Hemisphere
Southern Hemisphere
Sun
Northern Hemisphere
Southern Hemisphere
Northern Hemisphere
Southern Hemisphere

▶ The sun's rays strike New Mexico and the rest of the Northern Hemisphere at different angles as Earth revolves around the sun. As a result, the seasons change during the year.

DIAGRAM SKILL *What season occurs when Earth tilts so that the Northern Hemisphere is farthest away from the sun?*

The Sun's Influence

Earth's position in relation to the sun affects New Mexico in many ways. It produces day and night. It also produces the seasons of the year. The diagram on this page shows what happens when Earth revolves around the sun. To **revolve** is to move in a circle around a point. One revolution around the sun takes one year.

Earth moves in another way. It **rotates,** or spins, on its axis. Earth's axis is an imaginary line through the Earth from the North Pole to the South Pole. Day occurs when places on Earth face the sun. As Earth rotates, the sun's rays no longer strike those places. Then night occurs.

Earth's relationship to the sun also produces the seasons. You can see in the diagram that Earth's axis is tilted. As Earth revolves around the sun, the Northern Hemisphere tilts toward the sun for part of the year. A **hemisphere** is half of Earth's surface.

You also can see that New Mexico is located in the Northern Hemisphere. When the Northern Hemisphere is tilted toward the sun, that area receives more intense rays from the sun than areas tilted away receive. This causes the Northern Hemisphere to be warmer than the Southern Hemisphere. As a result, it is then summer in New Mexico and other places in the Northern Hemisphere. At the same time, it is winter in the Southern Hemisphere.

Earth's relationship to the sun also produces differences in climate. Areas that are near the equator receive intense rays of sunlight throughout the year. Because New Mexico is nearer the equator than places farther north, it has a warmer climate.

REVIEW What produces day and night, the seasons, and variations in climate?
Main Idea and Details

Geography and Climate

Before New Mexico became known as the Land of Enchantment, it was called the Sunshine State—and for good reason! New Mexico averages about 275 sunny days out of 365 days per year. This means that about three out of every four days are sunny.

All this sunshine makes New Mexico a generally warm and dry place in which to live. Differences in temperature and precipitation do exist within our state, though. Usually, places closer to the equator, such as the southern part of the United States, are warmer than places farther away.

Elevation can also have a strong influence on temperatures in New Mexico.

For example, temperatures in **Cloudcroft** average almost 20 degrees cooler in July than temperatures in **Albuquerque,** even though Cloudcroft is about 220 miles farther south. Why do you think this is so? The elevation of Cloudcroft is about 3,300 feet higher than the elevation of Albuquerque. Places at higher elevations usually are cooler and receive more precipitation than those at lower elevations.

For example, Cloudcroft gets almost 26 inches of precipitation yearly. Nearby **Alamogordo** receives fewer than 11 inches of precipitation yearly. Alamogordo is also about 20 degrees warmer in July than Cloudcroft. Why is there such a difference in climate in two places only 25 miles apart? Cloudcroft is nearly a mile higher in elevation than Alamogordo.

FACT FILE

New Mexico's Climate

Climate differences exist thoughout New Mexico. The information in the chart shows how temperatures and precipitation vary across the state.

▶ **Climate differs in Santa Fe and the nearby mountains.**

	New Mexico's Climate			
City	Elevation	Average January Temperature	Average July Temperature	Average Annual Precipitation
Raton	6,932 feet	30°F	67°F	15.4 inches
Farmington	5,625 feet	29°F	76°F	07.8 inches
Santa Fe	7,000 feet	30°F	71°F	13.8 inches
Albuquerque	5,326 feet	35°F	78°F	08.1 inches
Cloudcroft	8,660 feet	30°F	59°F	25.7 inches
Alamogordo	4,350 feet	43°F	80°F	10.6 inches

Sources: New Mexico Department of Tourism, New Mexico Blue Book, Western Regional Climate Center

▶ Like most of New Mexico's basins, the Jornada del Muerto is hotter and drier than nearby areas at higher elevations, such as the Organ Mountains shown here.

The Fact File on page 20 shows climate differences that exist among the state's regions. For example, very little precipitation falls in the desert basins. The mountains in northern New Mexico receive much more.

The Rocky Mountains region averages about 30 inches of precipitation per year. You can use a yardstick to see just how much water that is. In winter many of the highest places get nine feet or more of snow. That is about as high as the basket on a basketball court. Because of its high elevation, this region is also cooler in summer and colder in winter than most of the rest of the state.

Winters also are cool in the Colorado Plateau region. Summer days are hot, but nights are usually cool. Precipitation varies throughout the region. For example, mountain ranges may receive more than 20 inches of precipitation per year. Other parts of the region receive 10 inches or fewer of precipitation.

The Basin and Range region is generally the hottest and driest part of our state. Temperatures in summer can rise above 100°F. Although winters are fairly warm, temperatures may drop below freezing. Snowfall in the southern desert areas averages only a few inches per year. This region receives only about 10 inches of precipitation per year.

In the Great Plains region temperatures in the north average about 10 degrees cooler than those in the south. The southern plains also are drier than the northern part of the region. But they are not as dry as many places in the Colorado Plateau or in the Basin and Range regions. Next you will learn about how climate affects settlement.

REVIEW How does elevation affect climate in New Mexico? **Cause and Effect**

▶ Gila Cliff Dwellings National Monument is located near the Gila River in southwestern New Mexico.

Geography and Settlement

Throughout its history, New Mexico's environment has affected people's choices of where to settle. An **environment** is all the surrounding conditions and influences that affect the growth of living things. Climate and the availability of water are important parts of New Mexico's environment.

Our state's climate is one of its well-known features. New Mexico's dry air and warm temperatures have long attracted people from other places. Think about a typical summer day in Albuquerque. You have learned that three of four days in New Mexico are sunny. So on most days, people in Albuquerque wake up to sunshine.

However, even in July, temperatures in Albuquerque rarely rise higher than 90°F. Often brief thundershowers slow the rise in temperature. Usually nights are

pleasantly cool as the day's heat escapes rapidly from the land.

In winter, temperatures are generally above freezing around Albuquerque. Of course, at higher elevations winters are colder. With a climate like this, is it any wonder that so many people have come to New Mexico to live?

New Mexico's population has greatly increased in the past 20 to 30 years. In fact, the state's population is growing faster than the populations of many other states. Climate is only one of the reasons people are drawn to New Mexico.

The availability of water in the environment has been important in the settlement of New Mexico. Long ago early peoples settled near water. In Chapter 2 you will learn more about the people who settled near the Gila River. Today the homes of these early people are part of the Gila Cliff Dwellings National Monument.

Proximity, or being close, to water is important to New Mexico's communities today. Most New Mexicans live in river valleys such as the Rio Grande valley. Albuquerque and Las Cruces are located near the Rio Grande. Many towns and cities are located along the Rio Grande.

In parts of the state with fewer people, many of the towns are also located near rivers or streams. However, some of New Mexico's rivers and streams are dry for part of the year. The people who live in such areas must find another source of water. You will read more about New Mexico's water resources in Lesson 3.

Not all New Mexicans live in cities or towns. Some Native Americans live on reservations. Others live in communities called pueblos. *Pueblo* is the Spanish word for "village." Spanish explorers used this word to describe the Native Americans who lived in villages.

In areas of land farther from rivers, people may live on farms and ranches, especially in the Great Plains region. People in parts of this region are widely scattered. In Harding County, only about 800 people live in an area the size of the state of Delaware. Compare that number with Delaware's population of about 800,000.

The environment influences the choices New Mexicans make about where to live. Other environmental factors affect the distribution of plants in the state.

REVIEW How has New Mexico's climate influenced the state's population? **Cause and Effect**

▶ **Early peoples settled near rivers such as the Gila River.**

23

Plant Life in New Mexico

The different kinds of landforms, elevation, and climate in New Mexico's environment make the state home to many different kinds of plants. Plants and other living things are part of ecosystems. An **ecosystem** is a physical environment with its community of living things. Deserts are one kind of ecosystem in New Mexico.

At the lowest elevations, grasses and cottonwood trees grow along rivers such as the Rio Grande. In the deserts, cactuses and other plants are able to survive in a hot, dry environment. You can see some cactuses in the photograph on this page. Agave (uh GAH vee), mesquite (muh SKEET), and yucca (YUHK uh) are plants that also grow at low elevations.

The flower of the yucca plant is New Mexico's state flower. Native Americans have long used the fibers, or theadlike parts, of yucca leaves in weaving. Yucca roots were mashed and mixed with water to make soap and shampoo. Today some companies have adopted this traditional Native American practice. They manufacture and sell yucca shampoos.

High-elevation lands cover three-fourths of New Mexico. Many of the state's plateaus, foothills, and valleys lie between 4,000 and 7,500 feet above sea level. Various types of grasses grow in this environment. Juniper trees and piñon (PIN yohn) pine trees also are common.

The piñon pine tree is New Mexico's state tree. Piñon pine trees grow in almost every part of the state. The trunk and branches of this slow-growing tree often twist as it grows. Its roots help prevent soil erosion. On chilly nights people may smell piñon wood smoke from campfires or woodstoves.

Have you ever eaten piñon nuts? Piñon nuts are the seeds that grow in the pinecones of piñon pine trees. Piñon nuts may have formed one of the foods of the early Diné. Today the Diné and others still gather and sell the nuts. Many New Mexicans enjoy snacks of roasted piñon nuts or use the nuts in various food dishes.

▶ Most cactuses, such as the prickly pear cactus shown here, do not have leaves. The flat, round sections are part of the plant's stem. The pear-shaped fruit along the edges can be eaten.

▶ Forests of evergreen trees and aspens cover many of New Mexico's mountains.

Evergreen trees such as spruce and fir grow at elevations between 9,500 and 12,000 feet. Snow covers the ground for most of the year at these high elevations. When the weather warms and the snow melts, wildflowers burst into bloom.

At elevations just below 9,500 feet lie mountain meadows that are snow-covered for much of the year. Forests of pines and aspens also grow here.

Writer Ruth Laughlin once wrote about New Mexico's northern mountains in autumn. She described:

> "... quivering, flaming golden aspen leaves. Even where the pine and spruce are thickest, the flame of aspens shoots up between the evergreen...."

Over time, human activities have brought change to these natural environments. Farmers plow grasslands, and ranchers use them for grazing. Miners have changed the land by forming underground tunnels or open pits. Logging has reduced forests. Population growth has caused cities to expand. Houses now stand where none did before. All these changes affect plants and wildlife. So do the grass fires and forest fires that sometimes occur.

REVIEW What kinds of plants grow at the lowest elevations in New Mexico?
Main Idea and Details

New Mexico's Wildlife

New Mexico's different environments support many kinds of animal life. Bears, wolves, and cougars, also called mountain lions, are the state's largest predators. A **predator** is an animal that lives by killing and eating other animals. The black bear is New Mexico's state animal.

Wolves have returned to New Mexico after a long absence. A few years ago, the government released some wolves into the **Gila National Forest** in the southwestern part of the state. Like bears and mountain lions, wolves live in remote areas and try to avoid people.

People often see smaller predators such as coyotes and foxes in rural areas. To many people in New Mexico, the nighttime wailing of coyotes is a familiar sound. Coyotes can be a problem for ranchers because they sometimes attack young livestock. However, they are not usually dangerous to people.

Other animals in our state include elk and bighorn sheep, which prefer high mountain regions. Deer and pronghorn antelope live in lower elevations and on the eastern plains. Small herds of javelina (hah veh LEE nah) live in New Mexico's southwestern corner. The javelina has tusks and looks like a hairy pig with a long snout. Bobcats also are common in New Mexico.

FACT FILE

Official Natural Symbols of New Mexico

▶ State bird: Roadrunner

▶ State tree: Piñon pine

▶ State insect: Tarantula Hawk Wasp

▶ State flower: Yucca flower

▶ State animal: Black bear

Small animals such as chipmunks and squirrels can live in high elevations. A variety of snakes and other reptiles flourishes in hot, dry areas at lower elevations. Jackrabbits live throughout the state. Prairie dogs make their homes in valleys and grasslands. New Mexico also has large numbers of birds. These include ducks, geese, wild turkeys, and roadrunners. The roadrunner is New Mexico's state bird.

However, birds and other animals face challenges. As the state's population increases, people move into environments that animals need for survival.

New Mexicans enjoy the variety of wildlife, plants, and climate of their state. In the next lesson, you will learn about the state's varied natural resources.

___

REVIEW Which animals live in New Mexico's high mountain regions?
Main Idea and Details

Summarize the Lesson

- Earth's relationship to the sun causes day and night, seasons, and variations in climate.

- New Mexico's climate and geography affect where people live.

- Many types of plants live in New Mexico's environments, from deserts to high mountains.

- These many environments in New Mexico also provide homes for many different animals.

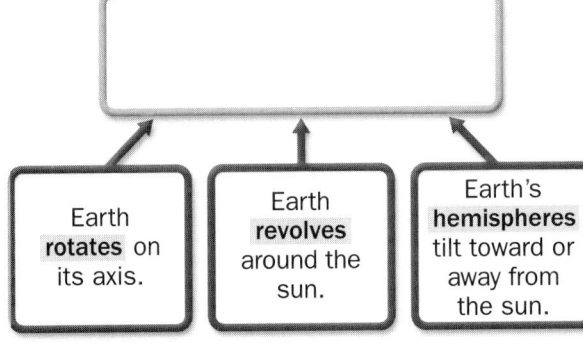

▶ Some New Mexicans call this animal a cougar. Others call it a mountain lion.

LESSON 2 REVIEW

Check Facts and Main Ideas

1. **Main Idea and Details** On a separate sheet of paper, write the main idea that is supported by the details shown below.

```
┌─────────────────────────────┐
│                             │
│                             │
└─────────────────────────────┘
   ↑           ↑           ↑
┌────────┐ ┌────────┐ ┌────────┐
│ Earth  │ │ Earth  │ │ Earth's│
│rotates │ │revolves│ │hemi-   │
│on its  │ │around  │ │spheres │
│axis.   │ │the     │ │tilt    │
│        │ │sun.    │ │toward  │
│        │ │        │ │or away │
│        │ │        │ │from    │
│        │ │        │ │the sun.│
└────────┘ └────────┘ └────────┘
```

2. Describe the climate of each region in New Mexico.

3. How has the **environment** affected where people live in New Mexico?

4. Identify the kinds of plant life that are found in New Mexico.

5. **Critical Thinking:** *Classify* List the types of environments in New Mexico, and identify the wildlife that lives in each.

Link to ⟳⟲ Art

Make a Poster Select and research an animal in New Mexico. Make a poster that tells about it. Include pictures of the animal, the region in which it lives, its environment, what it eats, and any human activities that threaten its survival.

Apply Information

What? Information is knowledge given or received concerning some fact or event. You get information from everything you see, hear, or read. Applying the information you have learned about something can help you draw a conclusion about it. A **conclusion** is a decision you reach that makes sense after you think about details that you have learned.

Why? Applying information is an important skill for understanding people, ideas, and events. Before making a judgment about something, you should first learn facts about it. Then you can use that information to draw an accurate conclusion. If you do not take the time to find out about something before you draw a conclusion about it, your conclusion may be incorrect.

How? Learn about the subject by gathering information about it. Decide which parts of the information are facts. Review the facts you have gathered. Use knowledge you already may have about the subject. Think about possible conclusions you can draw from the information. Think about whether the facts support each conclusion. Then choose the conclusion that makes the most sense.

Review your conclusion. Look for information that might make your conclusion inaccurate. Ask yourself what evidence supports your conclusion.

▶ **You can find information in reference books such as encyclopedias. Reliable sources of information on the Internet include government or educational Web sites.**

The piñon pine tree is important to New Mexico in many ways. The tree has a strong root system that holds the soil firmly and helps prevent erosion. The Diné boiled the tree's sap with sheep and goat hoofs to make glue. Piñon sap was also used in dyes and to treat wounds. Today the tree plays a role in some Diné, Pueblo, and Apache religious ceremonies.

Some New Mexicans burn piñon wood in their homes for its special scent. Others enjoy the seeds, known as piñon nuts, that come from its pinecones. They may eat roasted piñon nuts as a snack or add them to baked goods or main dishes. Piñon seeds are harvested as a crop. Many of the seeds harvested in New Mexico are sold outside the state.

▶ Piñon nuts are harvested from piñon trees in September and October.

Use information found in the article on the left to answer the questions below.

Think and Apply

1. What facts support the conclusion that the piñon pine tree plays a role in New Mexico's economy?

2. What conclusion can you draw about the piñon pine tree's role in the past?

3. Name two facts about the piñon pine tree that support your conclusion about its role in the past.

▶ The piñon pine tree produces seeds, or piñon nuts, inside its pine cones.

▶ Thousands of pounds of piñon nuts are gathered each year and sold in stores.

29

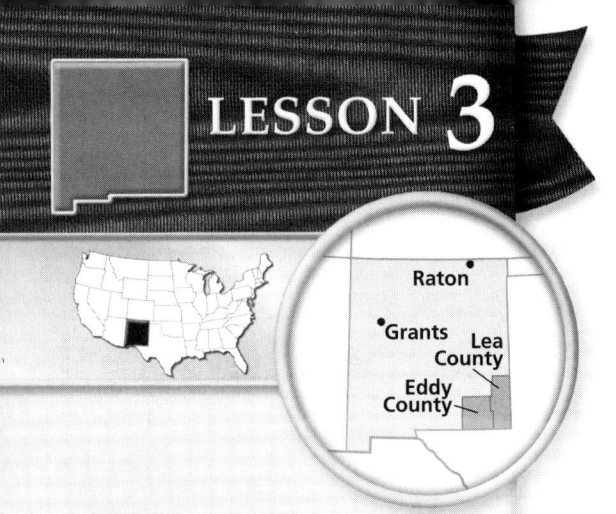

▶ Each calf is important on a ranch.

New Mexico's Resources

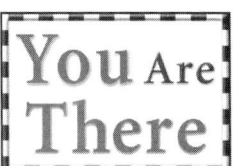
You Are There

Dear Diary,

Today was the fourth day of my visit to Uncle José and Aunt Betty's ranch. I am so tired! Today I helped Uncle José move some calves. Yesterday my cousin and I rode horses with one of the ranch workers to check the fence for places that might need to be repaired. We were out all afternoon. It was almost dark when we finally got back to the house.

I had no idea this ranch used so much land! It took hours to check the fence. I didn't know that taking care of the land was so important and so much work. I can't wait to tell my friends back home in Santa Fe about life on a ranch!

Summarize As you read, look for details that will help you summarize where natural and human-made resources are located in New Mexico.

Resources

New Mexico has natural and human-made resources. Natural resources include water, minerals, and soil. Human-made resources include farms and mines. The map on this page shows where various natural resources are found.

Some parts of New Mexico have fertile soil that supports the growth of crops. Soil in the Great Plains region supports ranching, and soil in the Rio Grande valley supports farming. Farms and ranches are examples of human-made resources. They produce livestock and crops for our food supply.

Minerals are an important natural resource in New Mexico. Mineral resources contribute to New Mexico's economy. Copper is found mainly in southwestern New Mexico. Coal is found in northern New Mexico. Later you will read about some ways they are used.

Water resources, such as rivers and lakes, are not spread evenly across our state. Human-made resources help meet the need for water. For example, dams have been built to create reservoirs. A **reservoir** is a place where water is

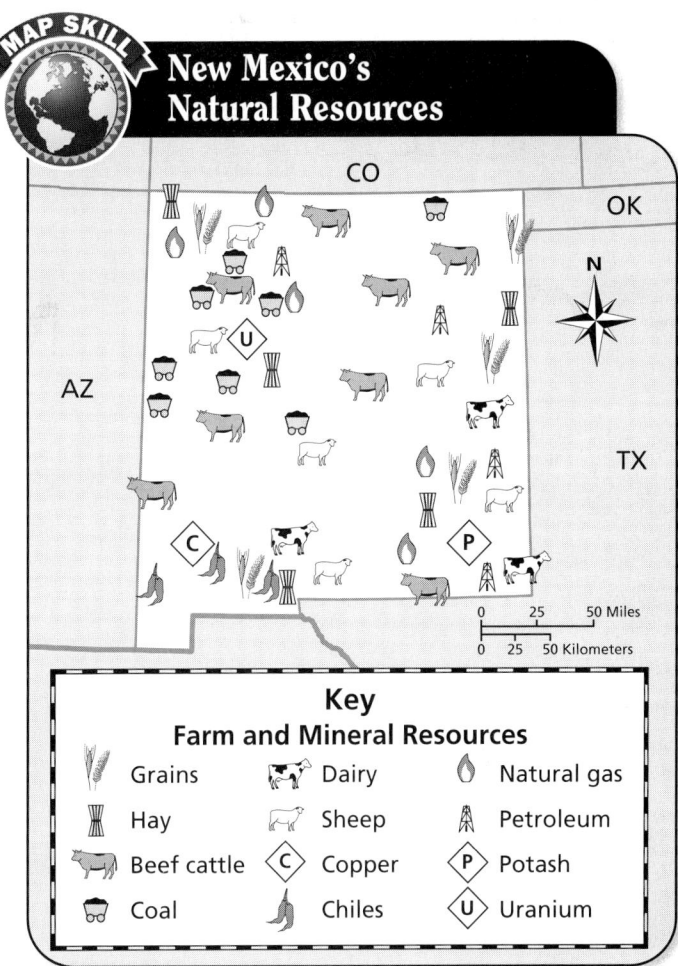

MAP SKILL New Mexico's Natural Resources

Key
Farm and Mineral Resources

Grains	Dairy	Natural gas
Hay	Sheep	Petroleum
Beef cattle	Copper (C)	Potash (P)
Coal	Chiles	Uranium (U)

▶ People in every part of New Mexico depend on the state's natural resources.

MAP SKILL Use a Map Key *In which parts of the state is oil found?*

stored for use. You will learn more about our state's water resources next.

REVIEW Summarize where natural resources are found in New Mexico.
🔁 **Summarize**

▶ Silver City was founded in 1876 by miners who were looking for silver.

Water

New Mexico receives an average of fewer than 15 inches of precipitation yearly. As a result, our state's limited supply of water is a precious resource. Rivers provide some of our water. Dams on some rivers have formed reservoirs. A dam is a wall built to hold back water or to control the flow of water from reservoirs.

Have you ever visited Elephant Butte Lake State Park near Truth or Consequences? The reservoir there collects water from the Rio Grande. This water forms the largest lake in New Mexico, and people go there to boat and water-ski. A few miles south is Caballo (kah BAH yoh) Lake, another reservoir on the Rio Grande that is used for recreation. Other reservoirs include Conchas Lake on the Canadian River and Sumner Lake on the Pecos River.

Water in reservoirs, rivers, and lakes is called **surface water** because it is on Earth's surface. Groundwater is another source of water. **Groundwater** is water that flows or seeps downward into the land. It soaks the rock below the soil and supplies springs and wells. In some places groundwater comes to the surface as a spring. In other places people drill wells to reach groundwater in an aquifer. An **aquifer** (AK wi fer) is a wide layer of underground earth or rock that contains water.

Rain and melting snow provide water for New Mexico's rivers, lakes, reservoirs, and aquifers. As the population grows, the demand for water increases. Ranchers, farmers, cities, and industries all need to use the state's limited water resources.

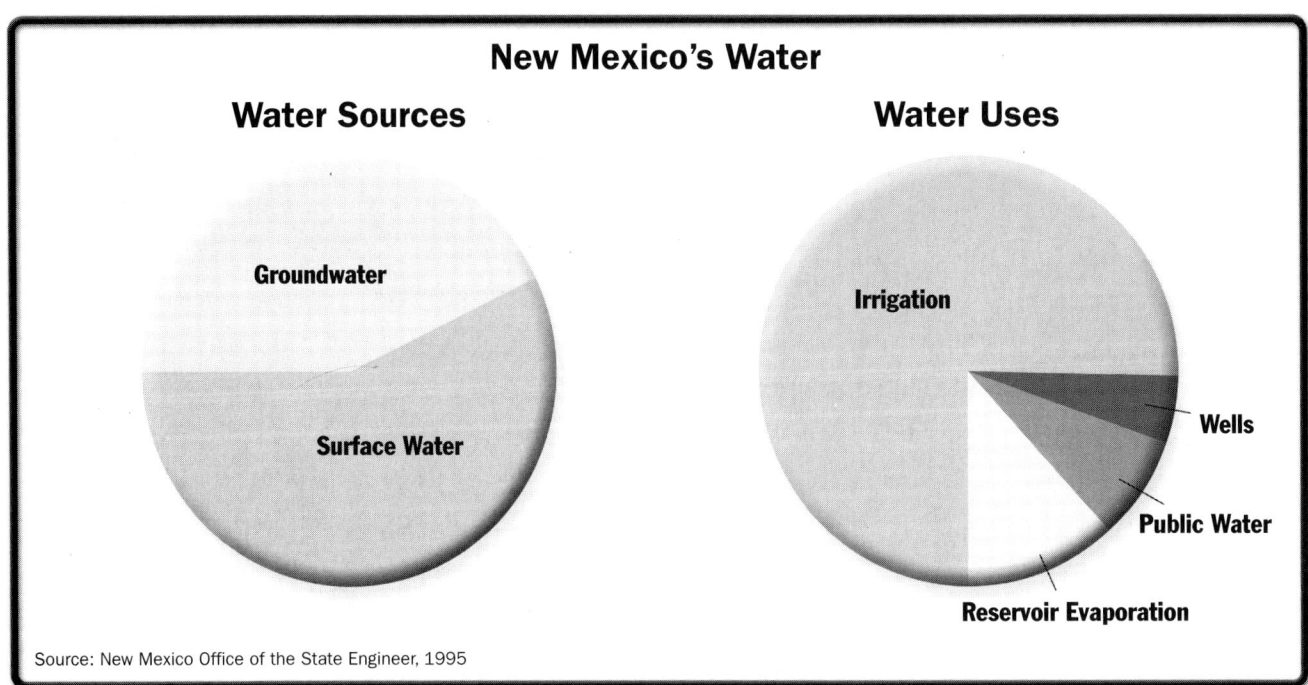

New Mexico's Water

Water Sources

Groundwater

Surface Water

Water Uses

Irrigation

Wells

Public Water

Reservoir Evaporation

Source: New Mexico Office of the State Engineer, 1995

▶ Groundwater supplies nearly half of New Mexico's water. Some surface water is lost when it evaporates, changing into a gas and rising into the air.

GRAPH SKILL *What is New Mexico's largest use of water?*

▶ Acequias are human-made resources. People in New Mexico
have used them over time to distribute water in communities.

The circle graphs on page 32 show the sources and the uses of our water. As you can see, most of our water is used for irrigation. In the Great Plains region, groundwater supplies most of the water for agriculture. In some other areas, agriculture uses more surface water.

Some farms and ranches get groundwater from wells or springs. Others use irrigation systems to move surface water. These systems use canals and ditches to take water from rivers or lakes to crops or livestock. For example, Elephant Butte Lake supplies many canals and ditches.

How is water distributed, or divided, among farmers and others who need it? Who decides how much each landowner receives? State laws usually determine water rights. However, in some places water rights were decided long ago. Early Pueblo peoples and Spanish settlers used acequias (ah SAY kee uhz). An **acequia** is a community ditch system that distributes water. Spanish settlers gave town governments the power to decide those water rights, or how water from acequias would be divided. Today state law requires that communities elect officers to manage the acequias.

The San Juan–Chama Project is a modern method of distributing water. Pipes and tunnels move water from the San Juan River into the Rio Grande basin. From there the water flows into the Rio Grande. In this way, the Rio Grande can supply more water to Santa Fe and Albuquerque.

REVIEW How does water affect the location of farms or ranches?
Draw Conclusions

33

Minerals and Their Uses

Mineral	Name	Location	Uses
	Mica	Throughout New Mexico; mined near Espanola	Used in wallpaper and paint
	Gypsum	Central and southeastern New Mexico	Used to make plaster, fertilizer, and paper products
	Pumice	Central and north central New Mexico	Used in concrete and cleaning products
	Potash	Southeastern New Mexico	Used in fertilizer and soap
	Uranium	Northwestern New Mexico; mined near Grants	Used to make nuclear fuel and as a dye in glass

Sources: Encyclopaedia Britannica, Columbia Encyclopedia, New Mexico Bureau of Geology and Mineral Resources

▶ Industries use New Mexico's mineral resources in many kinds of products.

Rich in Minerals

For years minerals have played an important role in New Mexico. Turquoise (TER koiz) is a sky-blue or greenish-blue mineral often used as a gem. Early Native Americans mined turquoise. They found much of it in an area south of what is now Santa Fe.

Years later people found copper, silver, and gold in southwestern New Mexico. Miners rushed to the area. Little mining towns such as Shakespeare and Black Hawk grew rapidly. When most of the silver and gold was gone, people left these towns. Today they are considered ghost towns.

Would you like to hunt for minerals like the miners of long ago? If so, you may want to visit Rockhound State Park near Deming. Ancient volcanoes scattered beautiful stones that are sometimes used in jewelry across the park grounds. There is no gold here, but you can keep any mineral you find.

Today copper is one of the key minerals in southwestern New Mexico. Only two states mine more copper than New Mexico. Our state still produces some silver and gold. New Mexico is the nation's tenth-largest gold producer.

New Mexicans have mined coal since the late 1800s. Most coal mines are located in the San Juan Basin and near Raton. New Mexico is the twelfth-largest producer of coal.

Copper and coal are not the only minerals found in our state today. As you can see from the chart on page 34, mica and pumice are also found here. Our state also is the top producer of potash in the nation.

Our state has the second-largest amount of uranium deposits in the United States. In 1950 a Diné shepherd named Paddy Martinez discovered uranium near Grants in the Colorado Plateau. His discovery improved the economy in that region. Many Native Americans and other local people got jobs in the uranium mines. Some land with uranium deposits belonged to the Navajo Nation, which was given money for allowing mines on its land.

New Mexico also has deposits of petroleum, or oil, and natural gas. Oil was first discovered here in the 1920s. New Mexico is the second-largest producer of natural gas in the nation. It ranks fifth in oil production. Oil and natural gas deposits are located in the San Juan Basin in the northwest and in two counties in the southeast— Eddy County and Lea County.

Each year New Mexico's plentiful mineral resources add billions of dollars to our state's economy. However, minerals are not the only benefit we receive from our land. Next you will read about how the land supports us.

REVIEW What kinds of mines and wells in New Mexico have provided jobs?
Main Idea and Details

▶ This oil pump is located in Eddy County near Carlsbad. It moves oil from deep underground into pipelines or holding tanks. Later the oil is made into gasoline or other products.

Fertile Land

Both ranches and farms contribute to New Mexico's economy, but they use land differently. Ranches require more land for grazing animals than farms need for crops. The average size of a New Mexico ranch is 3,200 acres. Farms in our state usually are small, with fewer than 100 acres.

Although farming uses less land than ranching, it needs more water for growing crops. Ranching is possible in many areas that do not have enough water for farming. In fact, our state has about twice as many ranches as farms.

Many New Mexico farmers irrigate, or bring water to, their crops. Early Pueblo peoples were the first to practice irrigation here. Sometimes they carried water from rivers to irrigate their crops.

Some farmers practice **dry farming**, which also began with early Native Americans. Dry farming uses only rainwater to grow crops. However, most places in New Mexico do not receive enough rainfall for dry farming.

Hay, cotton, pecans, chile peppers, and onions are major crops in our state. New Mexico is the nation's leading producer of chile peppers. The dry soil and abundant sunlight provide the perfect conditions for growing these plants.

The sale of livestock and farm crops is an important source of money for the state. Cattle and sheep are the main ranch products. In fact, more money is made from the sale of beef cattle than from any other agricultural product.

FACT FILE

Chile Peppers

Some people call them *chili peppers,* but New Mexicans use the Spanish name, *chile.* Chiles can be dried and ground into powder. Fresh chiles can be eaten raw or cooked in different ways, such as roasted. Chiles are used in many traditional New Mexican dishes.

▶ **Salsa is a spicy sauce made with tomatoes, onions, and chile peppers.**

▶ **Chile ristras often hang in New Mexican homes. *Ristra* is the Spanish word for the string that is used to thread chiles, onions, or garlic.**

▶ Cowhands on a cattle ranch still ride horses to check on cattle or move them to new grazing areas.

New Mexico's soil also supports the growth of trees. Forests cover nearly one-fourth of the land. In the early 1900s, our national government began working to protect forests, including New Mexico's, from soil erosion and fire.

Most forests are located in the northern and western parts of our state. Pine and fir are the most common types of trees. They are valued by New Mexico's lumber industry.

REVIEW How are farms and ranches alike and different in their use of resources? **Compare and Contrast**

Summarize the Lesson

- New Mexico's natural resources have influenced its people.
- Surface water and groundwater resources are limited in New Mexico.
- Many valuable minerals have benefited our state's economy.
- Fertile land supports ranching and farming in New Mexico.

LESSON 3 REVIEW

Check Facts and Main Ideas

1. ⟳ **Summarize** On a separate sheet of paper, copy the chart below. Write a summary of the details shown.

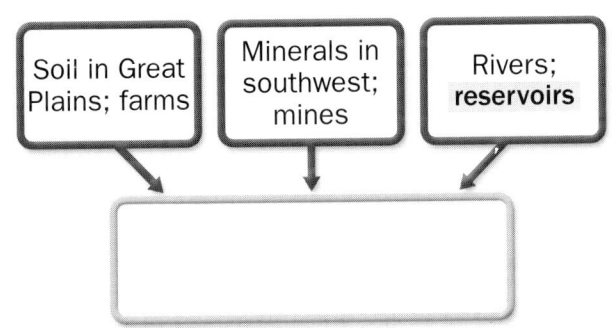

```
┌──────────────┐  ┌──────────────┐  ┌──────────────┐
│ Soil in Great│  │ Minerals in  │  │  Rivers;     │
│ Plains; farms│  │ southwest;   │  │  reservoirs  │
│              │  │   mines      │  │              │
└──────────────┘  └──────────────┘  └──────────────┘
        │                │                 │
        ▼                ▼                 ▼
        ┌─────────────────────────────────┐
        │                                 │
        └─────────────────────────────────┘
```

2. How does geography affect New Mexico's economy?

3. Identify minerals in New Mexico and their contributions to the economy.

4. Identify how farms, ranches, and the lumber industry contribute to New Mexico's economy.

5. **Critical Thinking:** *Classify* What are some human-made resources in the area where you live?

Link to ⟳⟳ Geography

Learn About Natural Resources Select one of New Mexico's mineral resources such as **turquoise.** Use reference materials to find out how that mineral was formed and why the state has so much of it. Prepare a brief report of your findings.

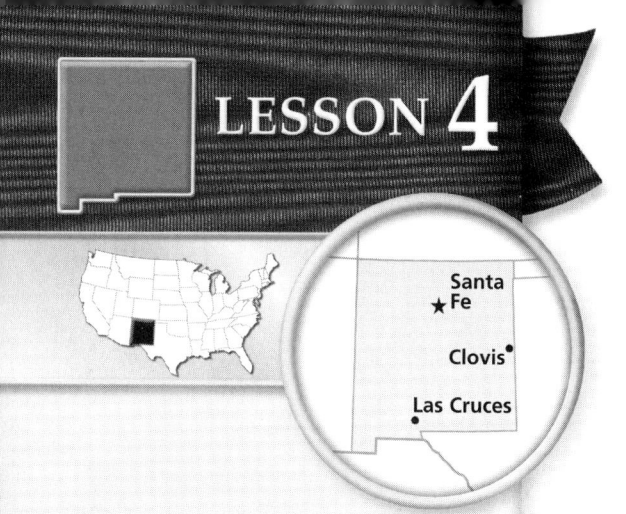

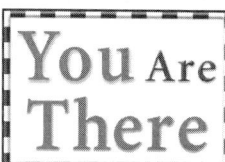

Focus on the Main Idea
People of many different cultures live in New Mexico.

PLACES
Clovis
Santa Fe
Las Cruces

VOCABULARY
architecture
suburb

▶ Photographs in family albums help keep family memories alive.

The People of New Mexico

You Are There Your parents have been telling you stories about how your ancestors came to New Mexico. Tonight after dinner you are looking at the family photograph album.

You can see how your town looked many years ago. There were fewer houses and buildings than there are now. The men and women in the photographs are wearing old-fashioned clothing.

You ask, "Where did they come from?" Your mother and father name a state far to the east. "They traveled a long way to get here," you say. "Why did they choose New Mexico?" You learn that your great-grandparents came because there were jobs in the mines. Other relatives brought their families because they could farm the land. You feel proud that your family helped New Mexico grow.

Main Idea and Details As you read, look for details that show the mix of cultures and communities in New Mexico.

New Mexico's Population

You have learned that New Mexico is the nation's fifth-largest state in land area. However, it has a small population for its size. It ranks thirty-sixth in the United States in population.

Natural resources affect where people choose to settle. People settle in places that have the resources they need to live. Resources are not spread evenly throughout our state. For example, many parts of New Mexico are dry. Many settlements in our state have grown near major rivers.

Even with challenges, New Mexico's population has grown steadily throughout its history. The graph on this page shows the growth in population from 1920 to 2000. In Chapter 3 you will read about the things that draw people to present-day New Mexico.

As you have read, New Mexico's population has grown faster than that of most other states during the past 20 to 30 years. Population experts expect this growth to continue. Next you will learn

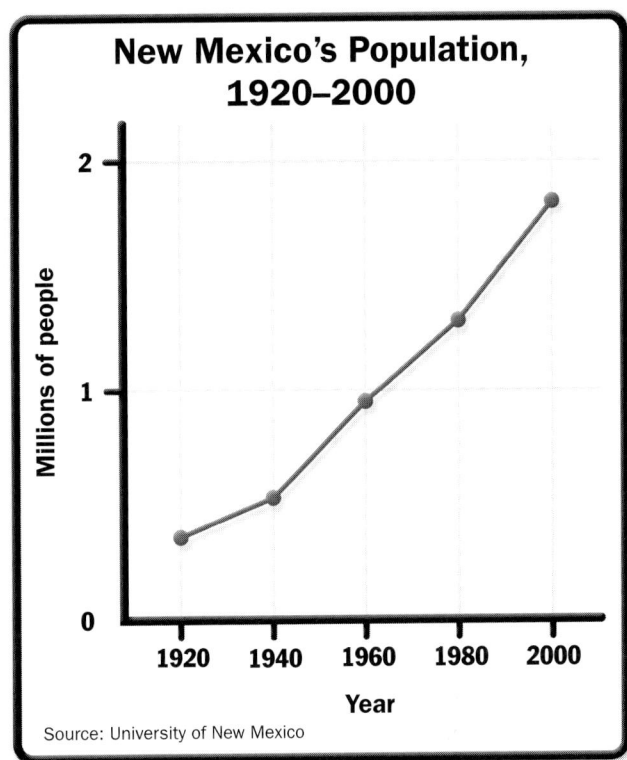

New Mexico's Population, 1920–2000

Millions of people

Year

Source: University of New Mexico

▶ New Mexico's population grew rapidly in the last 20 years of the twentieth century.

GRAPH SKILL *What was the population of New Mexico in 1960?*

about the variety of cultures that are part of our state's population.

REVIEW Summarize New Mexico's population growth over time.
⊙ **Summarize**

▶ Most large cities in New Mexico are located near rivers. Las Cruces lies between the Rio Grande and the Organ Mountains.

A Mix of Cultures

New Mexicans take great pride in the mix of people who call New Mexico home. Our state's population includes people of European, Native American, and Hispanic heritage. Smaller numbers of African Americans and Asian Americans also live here.

About one in every ten people in New Mexico is a Native American. Ancestors of today's Native Americans were the first to live in what is now New Mexico. Three main groups of Native Americans live in the state today. They are the Diné, also called the Navajo; the Apache; and the Pueblo.

The Navajo Nation, a huge reservation belonging to the Diné, stretches across parts of Arizona, Utah, and New Mexico. About one-fourth of this reservation is located in New Mexico. Most of the Pueblo communities in our state are located near the Rio Grande. Apaches also have reservation land in New Mexico.

Another part of New Mexico's cultural mix comes from the Hispanic population. Some people use the words *Latino* or *Latina* instead of *Hispanic.* A Hispanic is a person whose ancestors spoke Spanish. His or her ancestors may be from Spain, Mexico, Central or South America, or certain Caribbean islands.

Both English and Spanish are official state languages here. Many Hispanic New Mexicans speak both Spanish and English. Spanish words such as *pueblo* also often find their way into conversations in English.

Friendship and the exchange of ideas have led to a blending of all of these groups. This blend of different traditions helps shape New Mexico's culture. Almost any large gathering of New Mexicans will include a variety of names, languages, and kinds of foods.

▶ **These children from Isleta Pueblo are part of New Mexico's mix of cultures.**

The use of chiles, corn, and beans in New Mexican food also shows the influence of Native American cultures.

Many annual festivals celebrate New Mexico's rich culture. Among the best known are the Inter-Tribal Indian Ceremonial at Gallup and the Fiesta de Santa Fe, which celebrates Hispanic culture. Summerfest in Albuquerque honors a different culture each Saturday during the summer. Western traditions are featured each year at the Pioneer Days Celebration in **Clovis**, including a professional rodeo. The Smokey Bear Stampede in Capitan also offers a rodeo as well as a western dance.

The buildings in Albuquerque's Old Town provide more reminders of the state's Hispanic heritage. Some of these buildings are 300 years old. You also can learn more about New Mexico's Native American history at the city's Indian Pueblo Cultural Center. The center features crafts, art, and traditional dancing from the Pueblo communities in our state. In the next section, you will read more about the places where New Mexicans live.

REVIEW What are some festivals that reflect some of the cultures of New Mexico? **Main Idea and Details**

FACT FILE

New Mexicans Celebrate Their Cultures

▶ The Inter-Tribal Indian Ceremonial in Gallup features Native American dancers such as these from Taos Pueblo. The event also includes a rodeo where people compete in ranching skills such as calf roping.

▶ These dancers appeared at the Piñatafest parade in Roswell. This annual festival celebrates the influence of Hispanic culture in that city.

▶ People of all ages take part in the parade at the Old Lincoln Days celebration. This event in the town of Lincoln brings history and culture to life.

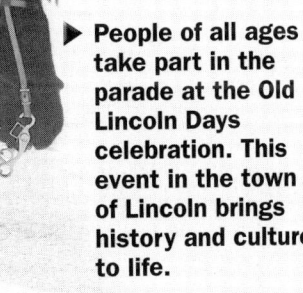

Where We Live

Nearly half of New Mexicans live in the type of settlement called cities. The chart on this page ranks some New Mexico cities by population from the largest to the smallest. You have learned that people often settled near rivers. This is one type of pattern, or arrangement, of settlement.

Albuquerque has a population of about 450,000, the largest population of any city in New Mexico. It is also one of the fastest-growing cities in the United States. Albuquerque is the business and industrial center of New Mexico.

Many houses in Albuquerque and throughout New Mexico are built of adobe

▶ Early people mixed earth and water to form a soft material called adobe. It was spread in layers to form walls. Pueblo peoples, such as this woman at Taos, later adopted the Spanish method of mixing mud and straw.

New Mexico's Largest Cities

City	Population
Albuquerque	448,607
Las Cruces	74,267
Santa Fe	62,203
Rio Rancho	51,765
Roswell	45,293
Farmington	37,844
Alamogordo	35,582
Clovis	32,667
Hobbs	28,657
Carlsbad	25,625

Source: U.S. Census Bureau 2000

▶ Albuquerque has more people than the other nine cities combined.

CHART SKILL *Which cities have populations of between 30,000 and 40,000 people?*

with flat roofs. Adobe is made of earth and water. Early Pueblo peoples used a soft form of adobe to build their homes. Later the Spanish added straw and formed adobe into bricks.

Architecture is the style or special manner of building. Adobe architecture is a reminder of our state's cultural history. It also shows people's connection to the land. Much of the soil in our state is ideal for making adobe. It contains the right amounts of sand and clay.

▶ Workers formed the mud and straw mixture into adobe bricks. They put them in the sun to dry. These bricks were used to make thick walls.

Santa Fe is the state's capital and government center. It is the second-oldest city and the oldest state capital in the United States. The city has been celebrating its Fiesta de Santa Fe for nearly 300 years. Santa Fe is also a major center for the arts. It attracts artists, writers, and musicians from across the United States and from other countries.

Las Cruces is an important agricultural center. It is home to New Mexico State University, which is well known for agricultural research. However, the United States government is the city's main employer. Many people in Las Cruces work for the national government at nearby White Sands Missile Range.

Suburbs are another type of settlement. A **suburb** is a type of community located near a large city. For example, Rio Rancho is a suburb of Albuquerque.

Some of New Mexico's other cities, such as Hobbs and Farmington, are smaller and farther from large cities. Military bases are important to the economies of Clovis and Alamogordo.

Clovis is famous as a place where evidence of early humans was discovered many years ago. In the next chapter, you will learn about the history of New Mexico's land and people.

REVIEW Why do so many New Mexicans live in cities? **Main Idea and Details**

Summarize the Lesson

- **New Mexico has a small population for its size, but population growth is steady.**
- **New Mexicans belong to many cultural groups.**
- **Nearly half of New Mexicans live in the state's cities.**

LESSON 4   REVIEW

Check Facts and Main Ideas

1. Main Idea and Details Complete the chart on a separate sheet of paper. Fill in the main idea that is supported by the details shown.

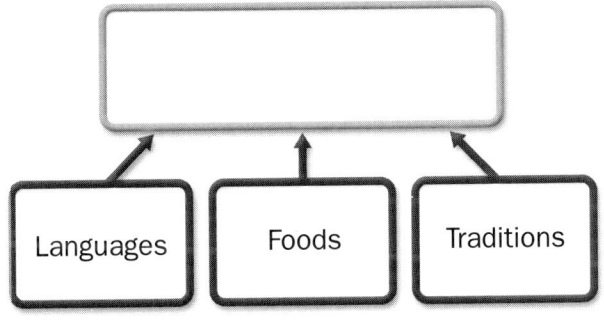

Languages   Foods   Traditions

2. Explain how geographic factors affect where people usually have settled in New Mexico.

3. Describe the different cultures in New Mexico and the communities they represent.

4. Describe types of settlements such as **suburbs** and how they are arranged in New Mexico.

5. **Critical Thinking: *Apply Information*** Which New Mexico city would you visit to learn more about the state's culture? Why?

Link to — Writing

Write an Article Select a festival that celebrates one of New Mexico's cultures. Write a travel article about the festival. Describe the purpose and history of the festival. Share your article with the class.

Chapter Summary

Summarize

On a separate sheet of paper, copy this chart and write a sentence that summarizes the details.

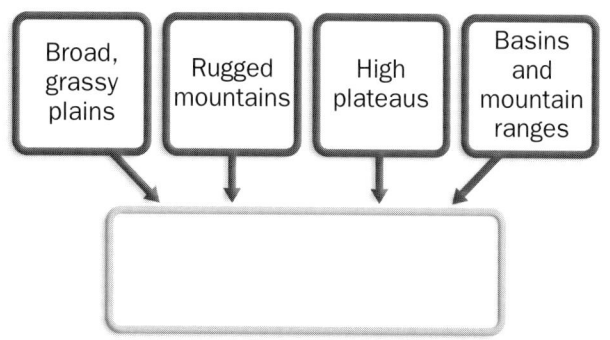

| Broad, grassy plains | Rugged mountains | High plateaus | Basins and mountain ranges |

Main Ideas and Skills

❶ Through which two regions does the Rio Grande flow?

❷ **Main Idea** Why is New Mexico home to so many different kinds of plants and animals?

❸ **Main Idea** How have minerals contributed to New Mexico's growth?

❹ **Main Idea** How might a visitor learn about the various cultures in our state?

❺ **Critical Thinking:** *Infer* Why do you think the population of New Mexico is expected to continue growing?

Apply Skills

Apply Information Review the information about the piñon pine tree on pages 24 and 29.

❻ Your school is planning to plant a new tree on the school grounds. What conclusion might you draw about choosing the piñon pine tree? Why?

Vocabulary and Places

Match each word with the correct definition or description.

❶ **mesa** (p. 8)

❷ **hemisphere** (p. 19)

❸ **reservoir** (p. 31)

❹ **acequia** (p. 33)

❺ **suburb** (p. 43)

a. a community ditch system that distributes water

b. a community located near a large city

c. a small, high plateau with steep sides and a flat top

d. a place where water is stored for use

e. a half of Earth's surface

Write a sentence about each of the following places. You may use two or more in a single sentence.

❻ Rio Grande (p. 10)

❼ Cloudcroft (p. 20)

❽ Albuquerque (p. 20)

❾ Eddy County (p. 35)

❿ Las Cruces (p. 43)

Write About New Mexico

❶ **Write a postcard** to a friend about your region of New Mexico. Briefly describe some of the area's resources, events, and attractions.

❷ **Write a travel brochure** about one of New Mexico's key cities or one of the state's natural landmarks.

❸ **Write an article** about the contributions of various cultural groups to life in New Mexico.

The History of New Mexico

CHAPTER 2

Lesson 1

Farmington

Scientists study ancient settlements near places such as Farmington.

Lesson 2

Taos

Spanish settlers made contact with Taos and other pueblos.

Lesson 3

Santa Fe

Santa Fe is the oldest capital city in North America.

Lesson 4

Glorieta Pass

The Battle of Glorieta Pass was one of the Civil War battles fought in New Mexico.

Lesson 5

Trinity Site

Atomic bombs such as the one tested at Trinity Site helped bring an end to World War II.

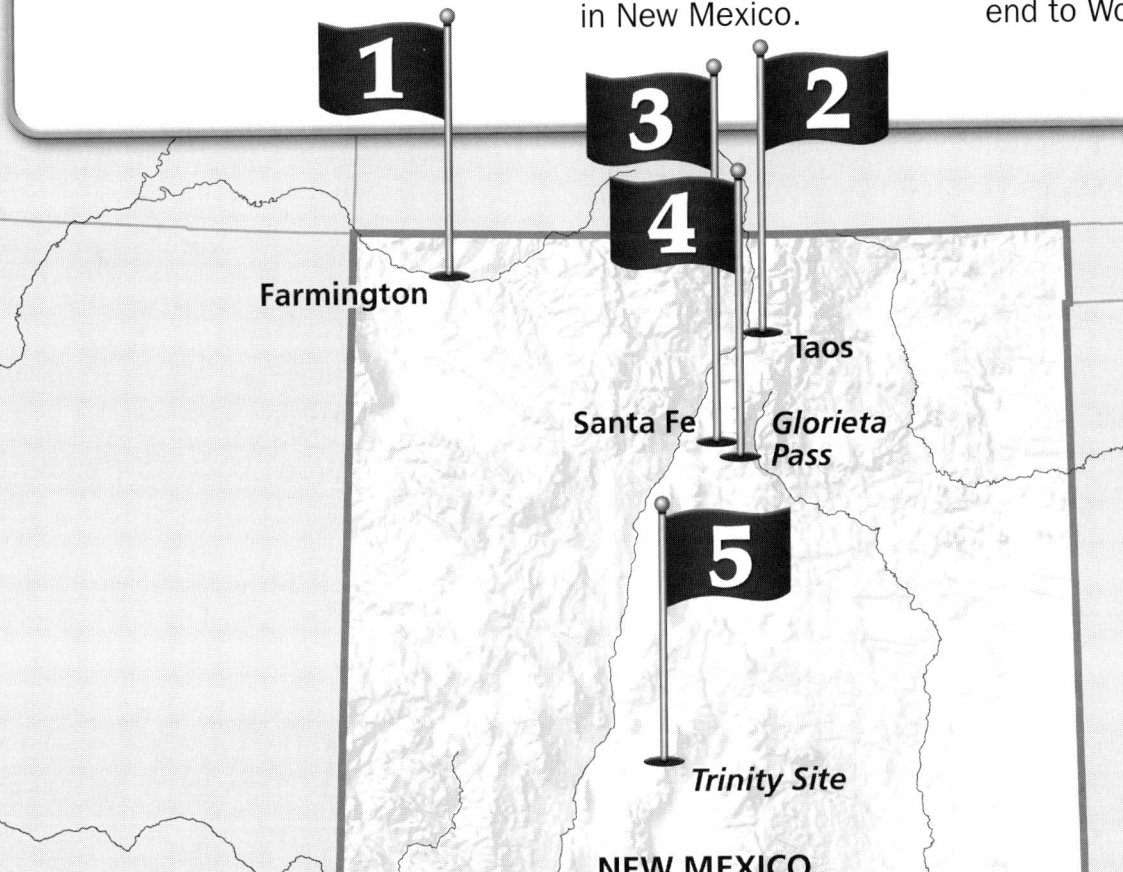

Farmington

Taos

Santa Fe

Glorieta Pass

Trinity Site

NEW MEXICO

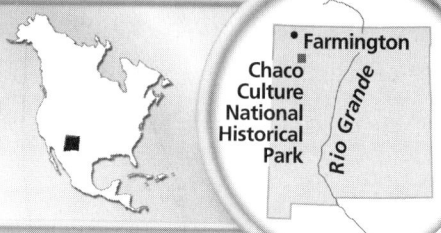

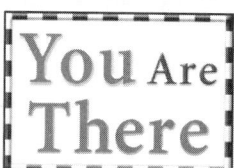

PREVIEW

Focus on the Main Idea
Early peoples in what is now New Mexico depended on the land for survival.

PLACES
Chaco Culture National
  Historical Park
Farmington
Rio Grande

VOCABULARY
archaeologist
historian
artifact
nomad

TERM
hunter-gatherer

▶ Skilled workers of long ago built walls of tightly fitted stones held together by mud.

Early Peoples

You Are There The park ranger leads your family and the other visitors along the path at Chaco Culture National Historical Park. The sun feels warm on your shoulders as you walk toward a large stone ruin called Pueblo Bonito. The ranger asks the visitors to guess how many rooms were there long ago. No one guesses the correct answer of about 800! The ranger tells you that this building may have been at least four stories high. Only the rooms on the ground level remain today.

You slide your hand along the closely fitted stones in one of the walls. You think about the worker who placed the stones so carefully and about the families who lived here. You wonder whether children played hide-and-seek around these walls so many years ago.

Main Idea and Details As you read, look for details that describe how people learn about New Mexico's past.

Clues from the Past

For a very long time, people have lived in the area we call New Mexico. However, early people did not write books about how they lived. We must depend on archaeologists (ar kee AHL uh jists) to learn about the past. An **archaeologist** is a person who studies buildings, tools, pottery, weapons, and other objects from the past to learn about people who lived long ago.

A **historian** is a person who writes about history. Historians learn about the past by collecting information through written records and other sources. Historians use this information to describe how important events have affected people and places.

An archaeologist uses artifacts to learn about the past. An **artifact** is an object that was made and used a long time ago.

Stone arrowheads and pottery bowls are examples of artifacts. Artifacts can tell the story of ancient places and cultures that existed before history was written down.

Archaeologists work where people once lived. They search for artifacts and the remains of ancient cities. The objects they find are like pieces of a puzzle. An archaeologist studies each item to learn more about early people.

New Mexico is rich in stories from the past. Archaeologists have studied the homes of early people in places such as Gila Cliff Dwellings National Monument. Archaeologists also have learned much about people who once lived in the **Chaco Culture National Historical Park** area in Chaco Canyon.

REVIEW What does an archaeologist use to learn about the past?
Main Idea and Details

▶ In Chaco Canyon, archaeologists have found artifacts such as tools made from stone and bone.

Early Peoples

Archaeologists have helped us learn about early peoples who lived in what is now New Mexico. Long before there were hammers or power drills, early people used artifacts such as sharpened stones or tools made from the bones of animals.

These early people were hunter-gatherers. **Hunter-gatherers** are people who hunt animals and gather wild plants for food. Some of these people also were nomads. A **nomad** moves from place to place to find food and other needed items. These early hunter-gatherers roamed the land for many years.

About 2,000 years ago, some groups of early people in the Southwest began to grow plants for food. They grew corn, beans, and squash. A steady food supply from farming made it possible for people in the Southwest to live in one place.

One of these farming groups was the Mogollon (muh guh YOHN). The map on this page shows that the Mogollon lived in the southwestern part of what is now New Mexico. They lived in round homes that we call pit houses. A pit house was made by digging a hole in the ground and covering it with a roof set on poles. About

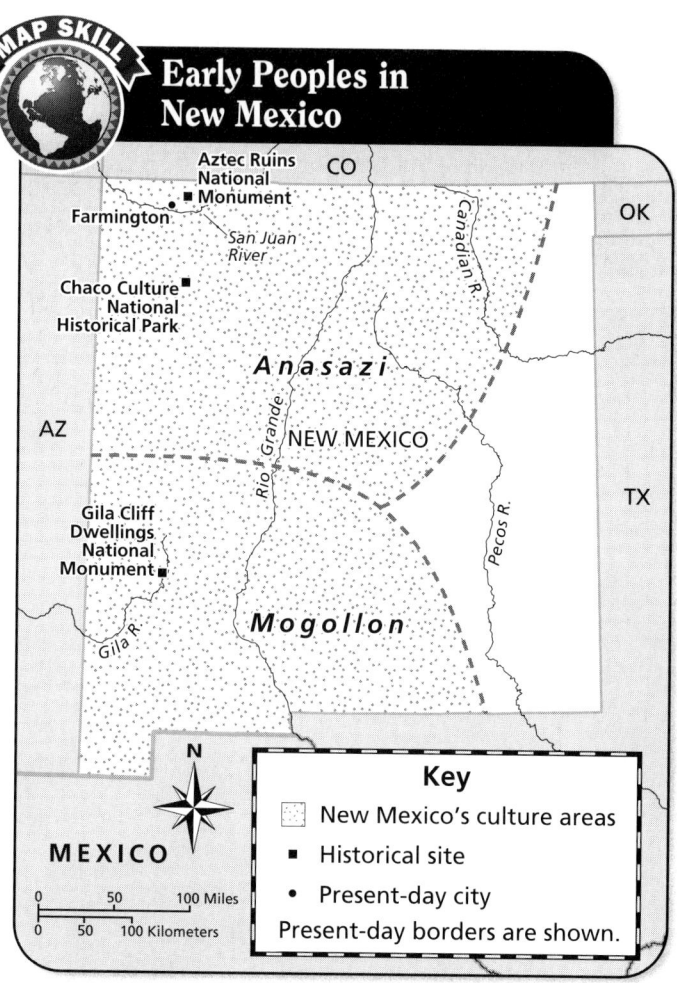

Early Peoples in New Mexico

Key
- New Mexico's culture areas
- ■ Historical site
- • Present-day city

Present-day borders are shown.

▶ Evidence of the Mogollon and Anasazi cultures has been found throughout the western part of present-day New Mexico.

MAP SKILL Use Cardinal Directions *What Anasazi site lies north of Chaco Culture National Historical Park?*

1,000 years ago, the Mogollon started building homes above ground instead of pit houses. These homes had many rooms, like apartment buildings. They also built homes in caves, such as those at Gila Cliff Dwellings National Monument.

At the same time, many other peoples moved into the area where the Mogollon lived. As a result, the Mogollon began to change their way of life. By about 900 years ago, they had blended with these other groups and were no longer a separate culture.

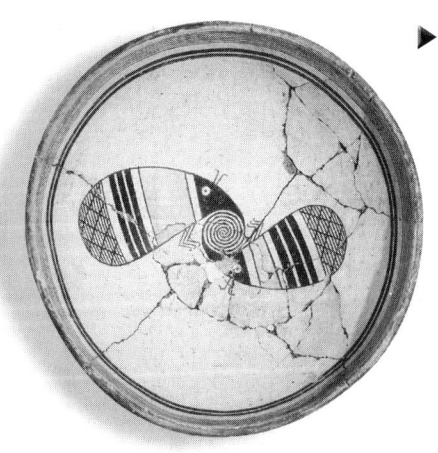

▶ This bowl is an example of Mogollon pottery. Mogollon potters stacked strips of clay to form a pot. Then they smoothed the clay and baked the pot.

▶ This Anasazi rock art shows an animal that the Anasazi may have hunted.

One main group that moved into the Mogollon's area was the Anasazi. The Anasazi lived in the northwestern part of what is now New Mexico. They had also been nomadic hunter-gatherers who began to farm about 2,000 years ago. They too built pit houses at first.

Between 1,000 and 1,200 years ago, the Anasazi made many changes in their way of life. They began to build stone buildings with many rooms and levels. Some of these buildings still exist at Chaco Culture National Historical Park, Bandelier National Monument, and at Aztec Ruins National Monument near what is now **Farmington.** The Anasazi also developed irrigation systems to move water from rivers and streams to their crops. They built many roads from Chaco Canyon to other Anasazi villages and places outside their area. These roads made it easier to trade with other groups.

About 700 years ago, the Anasazi left their homes. No one is sure of the reason, but some historians believe that a drought forced them to abandon their homes. They moved to different areas, including places near the **Rio Grande.** At each new place they built new villages.

The Anasazi who moved to the Rio Grande are the ancestors of today's Pueblo people. You will read about them next.

REVIEW What happened to the Mogollon about 900 years ago?
Main Idea and Details

▶ This drawing shows how Pueblo Bonito may have looked when people lived there.

▶ Pueblo Bonito is the largest ruin in Chaco Culture National Historical Park.

Pueblo Peoples

Three main Native American groups lived in what is now New Mexico when the Spanish arrived during the 1500s. They were the Diné, also known as the Navajo, the Apache, and the Pueblo.

You have read that the Anasazi are the ancestors of the Pueblo peoples. You learned that the Anasazi moved into the area around the Rio Grande about 700 years ago. Like their ancestors, the Pueblo built homes with many levels that looked like apartment buildings. However, these homes were made with mud, called adobe, instead of stone.

Because these people lived in villages, the Spanish explorers called them Pueblo people. *Pueblo* is the Spanish word for village. They also called the villages *pueblos.* Although people continued to use the word *Pueblo* to describe these people, they were not a single group. One group of villages may have spoken a similar language. However, four main languages were spoken among all the Pueblo villages. Pueblo peoples shared many customs, but each group developed its own history and culture.

Many of the Pueblo settlements were located near the Rio Grande. A few groups, such as the Zuñi, Acoma, and Laguna, had settled farther west.

The Pueblo people farmed, hunted, and gathered foods that grew in the wild. Water was very important to the Pueblo because they farmed in a dry climate. Many groups used irrigation systems to move water from rivers and streams to their crops. Some groups practiced dry farming, which you read about in Chapter 1. Pueblo peoples also practiced crop rotation, or the planting of different crops in different years.

▶ This photograph of Zuni pueblo is typical of homes built with many levels. The photograph was taken in the early 1900s, but this way of building homes is very old.

▶ A Pueblo family prepares food.

▶ The fireplace inside a Pueblo home provided warmth.

The Pueblo made many fine crafts. They shaped and painted bowls and jars. They also used turquoise to make beautiful jewelry. The hides of buffalo and deer provided material for moccasins. Weavers produced cotton clothes and blankets.

Pueblo men wore robes of woven cotton or the skins of animals such as buffalo or rabbit. Women wore woven knee-length garments that fastened at the shoulder.

Each person had jobs to do in a Pueblo community. Women ground corn, cooked, and made pottery. Men made tools, hunted, and grew crops. They also defended the village against attack from other Native American groups.

Religious ceremonies were a key part of Pueblo life. Some of these ceremonies included dances. Other ceremonies took place in underground chambers called kivas. People used a ladder to enter the kiva through the roof.

The Pueblo were already living in the Southwest when the Diné and the Apache arrived. These two groups probably came to the Southwest from what is now Canada about 1,000 years ago. Some historians believe that more powerful tribes pushed the Diné and the Apache into what is now New Mexico.

The cultures of the Diné and the Apache differed from those of the Pueblo and from each other. However, in some ways these two groups were similar. The Diné and the Apache spoke languages that were very much alike. Also, when they first moved into the Southwest, both of these groups were hunter-gatherers. You will learn more about the Diné and the Apache next.

REVIEW How did the Pueblo people get their food from the places where they lived? **Main Idea and Details**

▶ The traditional home of the Diné was a round, one-room dwelling called a hogan. It was covered in earth for protection from the weather. Some Diné still live in hogans.

The Diné and the Apache

You have learned that the Diné and the Apache spoke similar languages. In addition, both groups organized themselves in small bands that worked together to hunt and fight in wars. Their way of life included raiding other Native American settlements for food and supplies.

The Diné were nomads and hunter-gatherers when they came to the Southwest. By the 1600s they made contact with the Pueblo. From them, the Diné learned about farming. The Diné also traded goods with the Pueblo.

What might have happened at a meeting between the nomadic Diné and the Pueblo people? The Diné might bring hides and dried meat to trade. In turn, the Pueblo people could offer corn and blankets.

During the 1600s the Diné settled into more permanent communities. They grew fruits and vegetables. However, at times they still roamed the land to hunt and trade. Sometimes they raided Pueblo villages. They also learned to weave. Blankets made by the Diné became known for their beauty and skillful craft.

Unlike the Diné, the Apache did very little farming. They preferred to hunt and gather food grown in the wild. When food became scarce, they raided the Pueblo villages for food and supplies.

Because the Apache were nomads, they built simple houses. Their homes were built with poles and covered with tree bark or animal skins. These shelters were usually burned when the Apache moved.

The Apache frequently moved from place to place to gather food. They hunted during the fall and winter months. In addition, Apache men made their own weapons and scouted their surrounding territories for possible enemies. Apache

► **Young Apache men dressed for hunting**

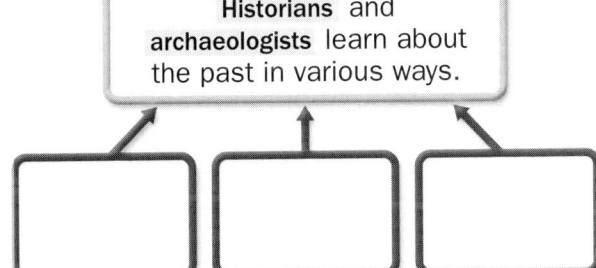

women handled the daily tasks of cooking, raising children, making clothes, and gathering food and firewood.

The lives of Native Americans changed when the Spanish arrived in the Southwest. As you will learn in Lesson 2, these changes led to conflict.

REVIEW How did the Diné supply themselves with food? ⟳ **Summarize**

Summarize the Lesson

- Archaeologists study artifacts and remains of ancient cities to learn more about early peoples.

- The Mogollon and Anasazi were early groups living in New Mexico.

- The Pueblo peoples lived here when the Spanish arrived.

- The Diné and Apache moved into the Southwest before the Spanish arrived.

LESSON 1   REVIEW

Check Facts and Main Ideas

1. **Main Idea and Details** Copy this chart on a separate sheet of paper. Fill in details that support the main idea.

> Historians and archaeologists learn about the past in various ways.

2. What important event happened about 2,000 years ago in what is now New Mexico?

3. Identify the ways in which the Pueblo peoples were connected to the places where they lived.

4. Describe the culture and communities of the Diné and the Apache and how they changed over time.

5. **Critical Thinking:** *Categorize* Which of the three main Native American groups in New Mexico were **nomads,** and which lived in permanent settlements?

Link to ⟴ Science

Learn About Farming Work with a partner to learn more about farming methods used by the Pueblo. Present your findings to the class.

1500　　　　　　**1600**　　　　　　**1700**

1532
Cabeza de Vaca's
group begins journey
through the Southwest.

1598
Oñate founds first
Spanish colony.

1680
Popé leads
Pueblo Revolt.

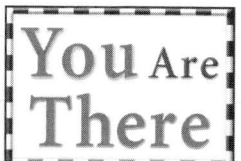

San Juan •Taos
★
Santa Fe

Spanish Explorers, Missionaries, and Settlers

PREVIEW

Focus on the Main Idea
Spanish explorers, missionaries, and settlers influenced life in present-day New Mexico.

PLACES
Taos
San Juan
Santa Fe

PEOPLE
Alvar Núñez Cabeza de Vaca
Estevan
Friar Marcos de Niza
Francisco Vásquez
 de Coronado
Don Juan de Oñate
Popé

VOCABULARY
expedition
migrate

EVENT
Pueblo Revolt

▶ Spanish explorers in the Southwest used spurs like these in the 1600s.

You Are There Standing in front of your home, you notice a cloud of dust on the horizon. A group of men appears, but you have never seen people like this before. The coverings on their heads and chests have shiny surfaces. Some of the men sit atop large animals with long faces and necks. These animals look nothing like the sturdy, square-headed bison you are used to seeing.

The men call out to you, but their words make no sense. What language are they speaking?

Sequence As you read, follow the sequence of events in the exploration and settlement of present-day New Mexico.

54

The First Spanish Exploration

Have you ever heard amazing stories about a place you have not visited? Explorers from Spain heard many legends about a land filled with gold and riches. One famous legend claimed that there were seven golden cities in what is now called North America. The explorers could hardly wait to see these golden cities.

In 1527 an expedition sailed from Spain to look for gold in Florida. An **expedition** is a long and carefully organized trip, usually made for a particular purpose. The Spanish explorers were shipwrecked on the coast of what is now Texas. By 1532 only four of the original 300 explorers survived, including **Alvar Núñez Cabeza de Vaca** (AHL vahr NOO nyez kah BEHZ zah day VAH kah) and an enslaved African named **Estevan** (es TEH bahn). Slavery is the practice of owning people and forcing them to work.

The four surviving explorers traveled toward what is now Mexico, which was then a Spanish colony called New Spain. They spent time with several Native American groups. Along the way, they may have been the first Europeans to see what is now New Mexico. During this journey through the Southwest, Cabeza de Vaca heard Native Americans speak about rich cities. They told him that people lived in huge houses with valuable goods.

Eventually, Cabeza de Vaca and his companions reached New Spain. Cabeza de Vaca's report excited Spanish officials. Other explorers in New Spain decided to try to find the seven cities of gold.

REVIEW Who may have been the first Spanish explorers to see what is now New Mexico? **Main Idea and Details**

▶ **This picture shows how an artist thought Cabeza de Vaca and his group looked. However, historians say that they had no horses and traveled on foot. In addition, their clothes were probably worn out. On their eight-year journey, the group may have walked more than 6,000 miles.**

Early Spanish Expeditions in New Mexico

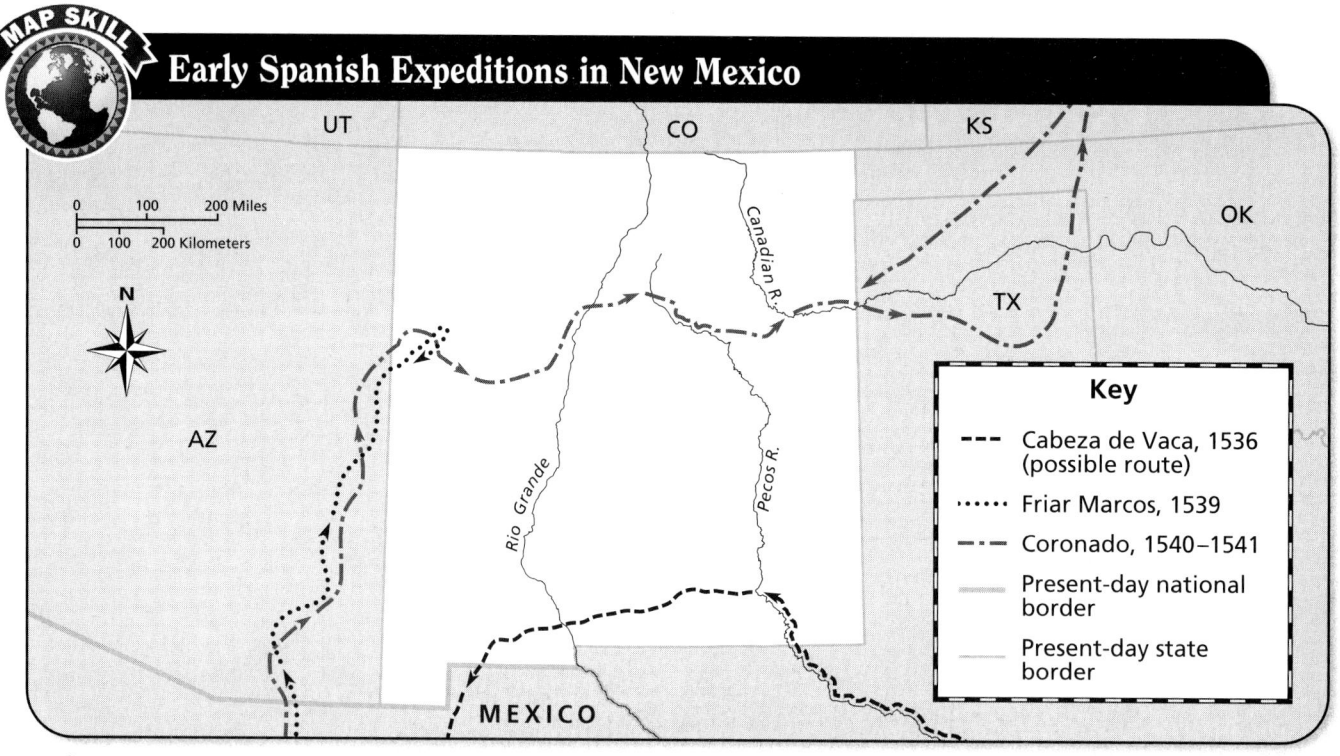

0   100   200 Miles
0   100   200 Kilometers

N

UT   CO   KS   OK

AZ

Canadian R.

Rio Grande

Pecos R.

TX

MEXICO

Key

- - - - Cabeza de Vaca, 1536 (possible route)

· · · · · Friar Marcos, 1539

- · - · Coronado, 1540–1541

──── Present-day national border

──── Present-day state border

▶ Spanish explorers traveled through what is now New Mexico during the 1500s.

MAP SKILL Trace Movement on Maps *Which three major rivers did Coronado's expedition cross?*

Spanish Explorers and Missionaries

For the next several years, expeditions searched the area Cabeza de Vaca had described in his report. Cabeza de Vaca chose not to go back there. Instead, a missionary named **Friar Marcos de Niza** (MAR kos day NEE sah) led an expedition. A missionary is a person who is sent into other parts of the world by a religious organization to spread its beliefs. His title, friar, meant that he belonged to a Roman Catholic religious brotherhood. Estevan went as his guide. The group set off to find great wealth and to spread Christianity to Native Americans.

You can see the expedition's route on the map on this page. As the group traveled northward from New Spain,

Estevan journeyed ahead as a scout. Friar Marcos eventually entered settlements the Spanish had never before seen. However, he did not find gold.

Although the expedition of Friar Marcos failed, people still believed the tales about cities of gold. In 1540 **Francisco Vásquez de Coronado** (frahn SEES koh VAHS kez day kor uh NAH doh) led five missionaries and 300 Spanish soldiers north from New Spain. As before, the goal of the expedition was to spread Christianity and claim wealth for Spain by finding the legendary golden cities.

Like others before him, Coronado was disappointed. He traveled as far north as present-day **Taos.** The Native Americans who lived in that village called it Braba. Instead of golden cities, the explorers found only adobe pueblos.

56

Many Native Americans did not welcome the expedition. Some tried to fight the Spanish soldiers. Finally, Coronado and his followers returned to New Spain without the riches they had been seeking.

During the late 1500s, other explorers and missionaries journeyed north through the Rio Grande valley. They went into parts of what is now the southwestern United States. One small expedition led by Friar Agustín Rodríguez (ah goo STEEN roh DREE gez) followed the Rio Grande to the pueblo villages. Antonio de Espejo (an TOH nyoh day ay SPEH hoh) led another group north to look for gold. Espejo was the first explorer to call the area "Nuevo," or "New," Mexico. The Spanish thought this area might provide mineral riches such as those found in "old" Mexico.

Over the next 100 years, missionaries worked among the pueblos. They built a network of missions and churches. Some Native Americans accepted the Christian religion. Some combined Christian rituals with their own religious traditions. Others continued to follow their traditional beliefs.

Relations between the missionaries and the Pueblo were often peaceful. However, sometimes the Spanish tried to force Native Americans to abandon their traditional religions. Later you will read about the conflicts that resulted.

REVIEW List the events that brought the Spanish into New Mexico in the order in which they happened. **Sequence**

▶ The mission at Taos was built in the early 1600s.

Spanish Settlement

Many of the Pueblo people had given food and supplies to Spanish explorers and missionaries. As more missions were built, Spanish settlement increased. However, the feelings of the Pueblos began to change when the Spanish began settling in the area.

In 1598 **Don Juan de Oñate** (DON HWAHN DAY oh NYAH tay) established the first permanent Spanish settlement in what is now New Mexico. Previous explorers had already claimed the area for Spain. The Spanish king appointed Oñate governor. Oñate organized a group of soldiers, their families, and several missionaries. They were the first Spanish settlers to migrate northward along the Rio Grande valley. To **migrate** means to move from one place in order to settle in another.

There were two main reasons for this migration. One was that the Spanish government wanted to spread Christianity among Native Americans. The second reason was that Oñate and the others wanted to find gold or other mineral riches.

Oñate supplied the group with livestock and building supplies. It was a long journey, and the group moved slowly. They started traveling from New Spain in January. In July, tired and worn, the people reached the pueblo of **San Juan.** It was located in a fertile valley where the Chama River flows into the Rio Grande. At first the Pueblo people were friendly and helped the settlers. Later, conflicts developed.

As the settlers began their work, Oñate, the soldiers, and the missionaries traveled to other pueblos. Oñate promised the Native Americans that the Spanish king would protect them from their enemies if they accepted Spanish rule. At the same time, the Pueblo people were expected to give the settlers corn and other supplies.

▶ Juan de Oñate was from a wealthy and influential family in New Spain.

Some Spanish Settlements, 1600s

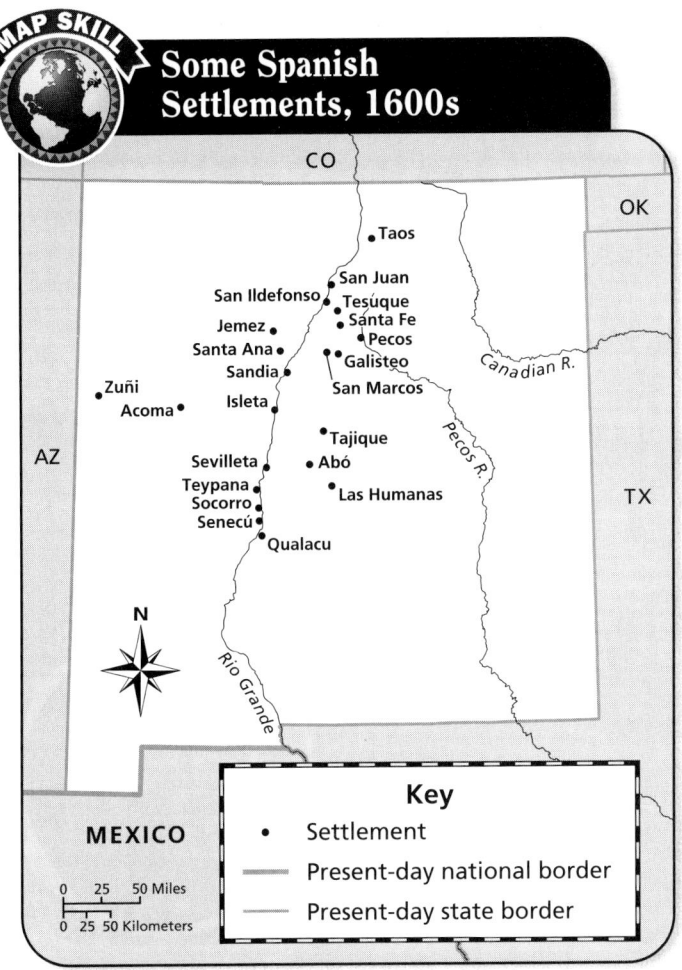

Key
- Settlement
— Present-day national border
- - Present-day state border

CO

OK

• Taos

San Juan •

San Ildefonso • • Tesuque
• Santa Fe
Jemez • • Pecos
Santa Ana • • Galisteo
Sandia •
• San Marcos
Isleta •

Zuñi •
Acoma •

• Tajique
Sevilleta • • Abó
Teypana •
Socorro • • Las Humanas
Senecú •
• Qualacu

Canadian R.

Pecos R.

Rio Grande

AZ

TX

MEXICO

N

0 25 50 Miles
0 25 50 Kilometers

▶ The Spanish located their settlements near existing pueblos. They wanted to spread Christianity among the Pueblo people.

MAP SKILL Human-Environment Interaction *Near what natural resource were many settlements located?*

▶ This type of plow was one of the tools brought by Spanish settlers for farming. However, many settlers were more interested in finding gold than in farming.

Before long the settlers at San Juan pueblo faced shortages of food and other goods. Oñate decided to tax the Pueblo. Each Pueblo household had to give the Spanish one bushel of corn and one small cotton blanket. When harvests were good, the Pueblo people could pay this tax. Sometimes drought or other hardships made it difficult for them to pay.

Late in 1598 a serious conflict occurred at Acoma pueblo. Some of Oñate's soldiers stopped near Acoma Rock. A few soldiers climbed the steep sides of the mesa to the pueblo in search of supplies. When the

soldiers reached the top, the Acoma attacked. Several soldiers died, including Oñate's nephew. A few months later, Oñate sent heavily armed soldiers with several cannons to Acoma. Hundreds of Acoma people were killed, and hundreds more were captured. The pueblo was heavily damaged.

The Spanish settlers were soon discouraged. No one had found any gold. They also worried about other Pueblo people nearby who might resist the Spanish. In 1601, while Oñate was away looking for gold, most of the settlers left. When Oñate returned, only a few settlers remained. He had not found gold, and there was conflict with the Pueblo people. As a result, in 1607 the Spanish king removed Oñate as governor. Three years later Oñate's replacement, Don Pedro de Peralta, established **Santa Fe** as the new capital of New Mexico.

Spanish settlement continued. The map on this page shows many of the Spanish settlements that were established during the 1600s. This increased migration to New Mexico resulted in more demands on the Native Americans.

REVIEW Why did Spanish settlers come to New Mexico? **Cause and Effect**

Conflicts between the Spanish and Native Americans

Oñate's defeat of Acoma pueblo made other Pueblo people afraid of opposing the Spanish. Tensions continued to grow between the two groups.

During the 1600s the Spanish worked to develop the colony. Missionaries continued their efforts to convert Native Americans to Christianity. Explorers searching for riches pushed themselves onto more land. In 1610 a government building was constructed in Santa Fe. The adobe structure was called the Palace of the Governors.

Throughout this period many Pueblo people were forced to work for Spanish landowners. A law established by the Spanish king required landowners to care for the needs of workers. However, many landowners ignored their responsibilities to the workers.

The Pueblo suffered other kinds of unfair treatment. They were forced to work long hours. The Spanish took some of the Pueblo land and used it for grazing cattle. Soil and water supplies were damaged. As a result, serious problems arose between the Pueblo and the Spanish settlers.

The Diné and the Apache also had conflicts with the Spanish. Both groups risked the loss of land to settlers. Both raided Spanish settlements.

Conflict increased during the 1600s. Many of these conflicts arose because

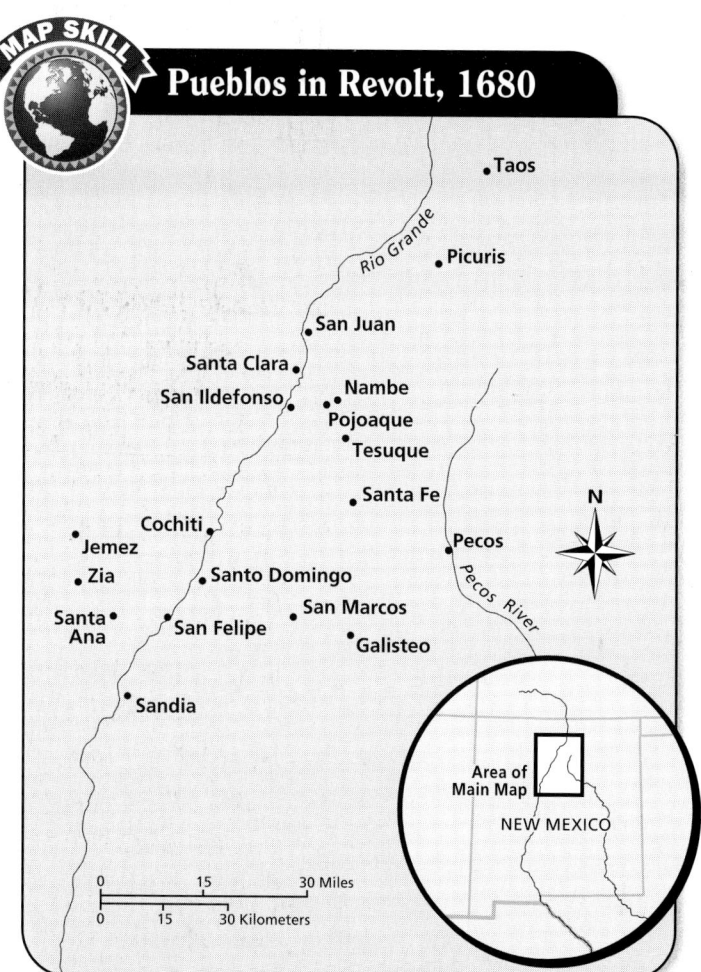

Pueblos in Revolt, 1680

▶ The Pueblo Revolt centered around the Rio Grande valley. The Zuni and Acoma pueblos in western New Mexico also joined the revolt.

MAP SKILL Use a Historical Map *Which pueblo on the Pecos River took part in the Pueblo Revolt?*

some of the Native Americans wanted to stop the spread of Spanish settlements and missions.

In 1680 the Pueblo man named **Popé** (poh PAY) from San Juan organized the **Pueblo Revolt** against the Spanish. Most of the Pueblo people joined together to attack the settlers and drive them out of New Mexico. By the time the Spanish heard rumors of the revolt, it was too late. Missions were destroyed, and hundreds of Spanish settlers were killed.

▶ During the Pueblo Revolt, Popé, shown in this drawing, encouraged the Pueblo people to return to their traditional way of life.

Survivors found their way to Santa Fe. They gathered inside the Palace of the Governors, the seat of Spanish government. The adobe building had walls that were four feet thick. After surrounding the capital, Popé released the remaining settlers. They returned to New Spain.

Popé had achieved his goal. The Spanish abandoned New Mexico. They would try to resettle the area, but it would be 12 years before they were successful.

REVIEW What happened during the Pueblo Revolt? ⟳ **Summarize**

Summarize the Lesson

1532 Cabeza de Vaca led the first Spanish expedition into the southwest.

1598 Oñate founded the first Spanish colony.

1680 Popé led the Pueblo Revolt.

LESSON 2   REVIEW

Check Facts and Main Ideas

1. **Sequence** Copy this chart on a separate sheet of paper. List these events in the correct order: Battle at Acoma Pueblo; Pueblo Revolt; Santa Fe becomes the capital; Coronado's expedition.

> 1540
> ↓
> 1598
> ↓
> 1610
> ↓
> 1680

2. Explain how Spanish explorers and missionaries changed the lives of Native Americans.

3. Identify the reasons why the Spanish migrated to New Mexico.

4. Identify the important event that drove the Spanish out of New Mexico, and name the person who organized it.

5. **Critical Thinking: *Predict*** What do you think might have happened if Spanish settlers had found gold?

Link to ⟷ Art

Design a Poster Design a poster that might have been used by the government of Spain to persuade people to settle in New Mexico. Include drawings and captions that describe what the settlers might find.

1650   1750   1850

1692
Spanish return
to New Mexico.

1821
Mexico controls
New Mexico.

1850
New Mexico
becomes a
U.S. territory.

Santa Fe
Trail

El Camino
Real

★ Santa Fe
Albuquerque

PREVIEW

Focus on the Main Idea
New Mexico has been governed by Spain, Mexico, and the United States.

PLACES
Santa Fe
Albuquerque
El Camino Real
Santa Fe Trail

PEOPLE
Don Diego de Vargas
Zebulon Pike
William Becknell
Susan Shelby Magoffin

VOCABULARY
territory

TERM
land grant

EVENTS
Mexican War
Treaty of Guadalupe Hidalgo
Compromise of 1850

▶ Carts such as this one were used in Spanish colonial times.

Spanish and Mexican Rule

You Are There

Dear Diary,
 Tomorrow is the day we start out! Everyone in our group of settlers is taking food, clothing, tools, and cooking pots. It will take a long time to reach the settlement. Along the way we will stop each night and make camp. I think it will be fun to eat dinner outside in the open air.

 My parents tell me that the settlement is near a river called the Rio Grande. Its wide valley is a good place to farm. There are mountains in the distance. At night we will hear the coyotes singing to the moon and stars.

 There will be a lot of work to do when we get there, but I am ready. New Mexico, here we come!

Sequence As you read, trace the order of events in Santa Fe when the Spanish returned.

The Spanish Return

After the Pueblo Revolt, the Spanish tried unsuccessfully to recapture New Mexico. In November 1681, soldiers returned to the area. They took control of a few pueblos. When they neared Santa Fe, Pueblo warriors were waiting. The Spanish troops decided not to fight. They retreated to the south.

However, the Spanish still claimed New Mexico. They wanted to regain control of the area. They did not always respect the human rights, or freedom, of the Pueblo. You have learned that the Spanish controlled lands where the Pueblo lived and taxed them. In 1690 Don Diego de Vargas was appointed governor of New Mexico. He was supposed to organize a group of soldiers and lead them north along the Rio Grande.

In 1692 de Vargas and the soldiers reached Santa Fe, but the Pueblo people refused to allow them to enter. De Vargas told the Pueblo people that he did not want to fight. Instead, he welcomed them as part of Spain.

The Pueblo people were facing Spanish troops. Their leader Popé had died, and they were troubled by the Apache. Finally the Pueblo surrendered. De Vargas then traveled to many other pueblos, which also surrendered. Once again New Mexico was under Spanish control.

Unfortunately, the peace did not last long. De Vargas left for New Spain to bring new settlers and missionaries to New Mexico. In late 1693 they returned. The Pueblo had changed their minds, and they no longer were willing to welcome the Spanish. They may have been thinking of how the Spanish had treated them in the past. As a result, de Vargas had to take Santa Fe by force.

The Pueblo people fought the Spanish now and then for the next few years, but resistance finally ended. The missions reopened, and Spanish settlements grew.

REVIEW How did de Vargas treat the Pueblo people at Santa Fe on his first trip? **Main Idea and Details**

▶ Don Diego de Vargas was eager to regain control of New Mexico for Spain.

Life in Spanish Settlements

By the early 1700s, the number of Spanish settlements increased in New Mexico. Most of the earlier settlements were located near the Rio Grande. In 1706 settlers founded **Albuquerque** on the Rio Grande. It became a key settlement south of Santa Fe.

Life in a Spanish settlement during the 1700s was filled with a variety of sights, sounds, and smells. Spanish ranch houses and their courtyards often were filled with activity. A courtyard is a space enclosed by walls, in or near a large building. Inside the home you could sit down to a meal of meat and corn that had been roasted over an open fire. Outside, you could see sheep, goats, horses, and burros. *Burro* is the Spanish word for donkey. You also could see irrigation ditches channeling precious water to the crops in the fields.

Buildings served various purposes. Some had storage rooms that held dried herbs, fruits, and vegetables. Settlers depended on this food until the next harvest. A larger ranch might also have its own chapel. A chapel is a building for worship that is not quite as large as a church.

In addition to farm work, Spanish settlers also worked at crafts. Weavers used thread spun from sheep's wool to weave clothing, blankets, and rugs.

As New Mexico's population grew, people settled on land farther away from the Rio Grande. The Spanish king gave land to people as a reward. These gifts of land were call **land grants.** Some land grants were given for land near the Rio Grande, but many others gave land that was much farther away. People built houses and farms on the land. Sometimes settlements grew from land grants.

▶ Around 1775 an artist painted this picture of a family in a Spanish settlement.

64

These settlements far from the Rio Grande also were far from one another. As a result, people there faced greater danger from the Diné, the Ute (YOOT), the Apache, and from the Comanche (kuh MAN chee), another Native American group. The Comanche were hunters who had lived in what is now Wyoming. They moved into New Mexico in the 1700s. They often raided settlements.

One road connected settlements from the south to the north. This road was called **El Camino Real** (EL cah MEE noh RAY al), or the Royal Road. Traders and settlers followed this route from Mexico City, the capital of the Spanish colony of New Spain, up to the Rio Grande and north to Santa Fe and Taos. Traders brought household items, tools, supplies, and news from Mexico.

Travelers on El Camino Real faced a long and sometimes dangerous trip. The journey took months, and the road passed through harsh deserts. There was also a risk of attack by the Apache or the Comanche.

REVIEW What kind of work was done in a Spanish settlement in the 1700s? ⟳ **Summarize**

FACT FILE

Spanish Influences in New Mexico

Today Spanish influences can still be seen throughout our state.

▶ Mariachi bands use instruments brought by the Spanish, such as violins, guitars, and horns.

▶ A serape is a woven blanket that Spanish men sometimes wore as a coat.

▶ Horses were first brought to New Mexico by the Spanish.

▶ A stringed instrument similar to the modern guitar was used in Spain as early as the 1500s.

65

Challenges and Growth

During the time that the Spanish settled the Southwest, the French claimed other parts of North America. The map on this page shows the land each of these countries claimed.

In the early 1700s, French traders began doing business with settlers in New Mexico. Spanish officials did not want traders from other countries to earn money in New Mexico. They declared that only Spanish traders could sell goods to settlers in New Mexico. However, when French traders entered Santa Fe in the 1740s, the settlers ignored the rule and traded with them. They bought French goods such as cloth.

During this time, some Native American groups attacked the Spanish. Groups of Ute, Diné, Apache, and Comanche led raids against the Spanish settlers. These groups also raided the Pueblo villages. They took livestock and other goods and supplies.

In 1786 the Spanish finally persuaded the Comanche and the Ute to agree to a peace treaty. Both groups and the Spanish governor promised an end to war. In fact, the Comanche, Ute, and Pueblo helped the Spanish battle Apache and Diné raiders. People continued to settle in New Mexico, and the Spanish population grew steadily.

Meanwhile, important events were occurring in the eastern part of North America. The 13 British colonies declared their independence in 1776 and won the Revolutionary War. The fighting ended in

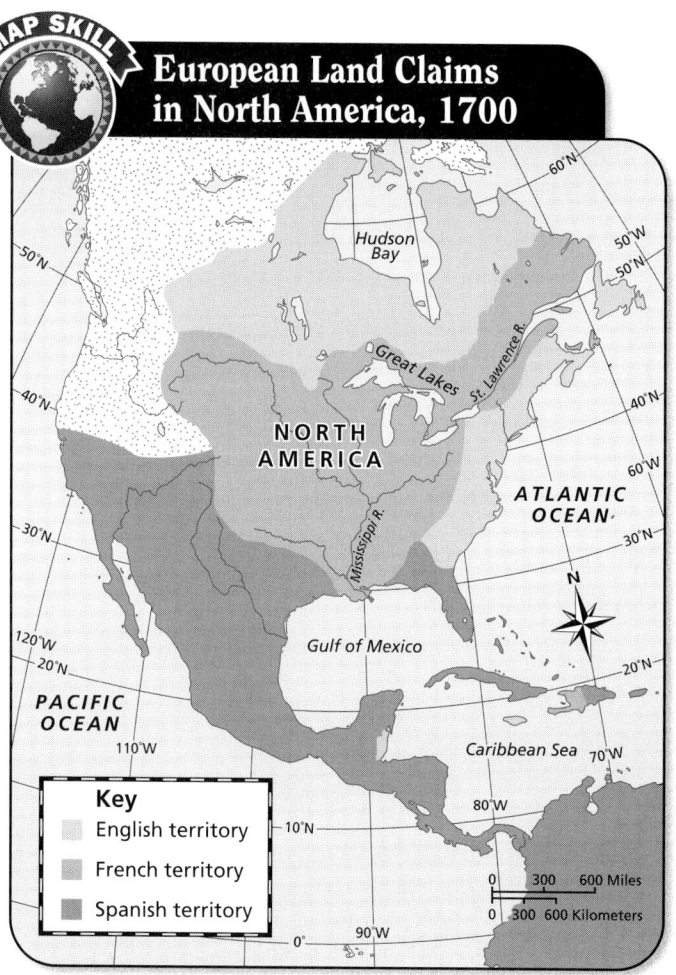

European Land Claims in North America, 1700

Key
- English territory
- French territory
- Spanish territory

▶ French land claims in North America bordered Spanish land claims.

MAP SKILL Understand Directions *What body of water lies on the western border of Spanish territory in North America?*

1781, and a peace treaty was signed in 1783. These events marked the beginning of the United States of America.

Soon the Spanish had another reason to worry. In 1803 the United States bought the Louisiana Territory from France. The Louisiana Territory was the large area of land between the Mississippi River, Rocky Mountains, Canada, and the Gulf of Mexico. The Spanish feared a growing United States. A larger United States might threaten Spain's hold on New Mexico.

The United States government was eager to learn about the area west of the Mississippi River. President Thomas Jefferson decided to send an expedition to explore the West. Meriwether Lewis and William Clark began their exploration of the Louisiana Territory in 1804. Lewis and Clark's route along the Missouri River took them closer to New Mexico than Americans had been before.

In 1806 **Zebulon Pike** led an another expedition to explore the Louisiana Purchase. Pike was exploring the Rocky Mountains. In 1807, Pike and his group crossed into New Mexico. The Spanish forced Pike to leave.

Later Pike wrote a book about his journey. He described New Mexico as a place with opportunities. United States traders became interested in New Mexico. Next you will learn how trade grew when New Mexico's government changed.

REVIEW Did the first French traders arrive in Santa Fe before or after Zebulon Pike did? **Sequence**

▶ An artist painted this picture of Zebulon Pike and his group. The Spanish pictured here captured Pike in northern New Mexico. They took him and his group to Santa Fe, then into Mexico, and then into Louisiana before finally releasing them.

Mexican Rule

New Spain had been a Spanish colony for a long time. New Spain was the name for the land that is now Mexico. New Mexico was the northern part of that colony. Its governors came from New Spain. However, in 1821 New Spain declared independence from Spain, becoming the new country of Mexico. New Mexico then became a part of Mexico. The Mexican government ruled New Mexico for the next 25 years.

Unlike Spain, Mexico allowed traders to do business in New Mexico. In the early 1820s, a trader from Missouri named **William Becknell** arrived in Santa Fe. He had brought goods from Missouri to sell. Becknell sold so much that he came back the next year with more goods. The route he followed from Missouri to New Mexico became a major trade route called the **Santa Fe Trail.**

A few years later, **Susan Shelby Magoffin** (mah GOF in) traveled with her husband on a trading trip. She was one of the first American women to travel the Santa Fe Trail. She enjoyed a feeling of freedom during the journey. Along the way she kept a detailed journal. She wrote,

"I breathe free without that oppression [bad treatment] and uneasiness felt in the gossiping groups of a settled home."

The appointment of Albino Pérez (ahl BEE noh PE rez) as governor of New Mexico brought new conflict. Pérez tried to increase taxes, and New Mexican settlers rebelled against him in 1837. Pérez was killed, and Manuel Armijo (MAH nwel ar MEE hoh) became the next governor of New Mexico.

For some time, relations between New Mexico and its neighbor, the independent Republic of Texas, had been uneasy. Both claimed land east of the Rio Grande. Then in 1841 a group of traders and soldiers from Texas traveled to New Mexico.

▶ Traders on the Santa Fe Trail traveled in groups of up to 100 wagons pulled by oxen or mules. This picture shows them arriving at the plaza in Santa Fe. The cottonwood trees were planted by Santa Fe citizens.

Members of the Texas group said that they wanted to take part in trade at Santa Fe. Governor Armijo believed that they were invading. It is not certain what the Texans wanted. Armijo led some troops eastward and met the Texans. Armijo's New Mexico troops forced the Texans to leave.

Texas became part of the United States in 1845. Mexico was angered by this event. This anger turned to conflict in 1846, when the **Mexican War** began. The United States battled Mexico over the boundary of Texas. Mexico claimed the boundary was the Nueces River. The United States claimed it was the Rio Grande.

In 1848 the **Treaty of Guadalupe Hidalgo** ended the Mexican War. The treaty established the boundary between the United States and Mexico along the Rio Grande and the Gila River. As a result of the treaty, the United States paid Mexico for its territory in New Mexico.

REVIEW How did Mexico govern New Mexico differently from the way Spain had governed it? **Compare and Contrast**

Map Adventure

The Santa Fe Trail and El Camino Real

You live in Santa Fe. It is exciting when traders arrive at the plaza with goods they have brought along the Santa Fe Trail. Other traders travel from Mexico along El Camino Real.

Use the map to answer the questions.

1. Two traders travel west from Independence on the Santa Fe Trail. One takes the Mountain Route. The other takes the Cimarron Route. Where do the traders next meet?

2. Some traders travel on El Camino Real from Mexico. What river do they cross as they enter New Mexico?

3. In which direction do traders travel to go from El Paso to Santa Fe?

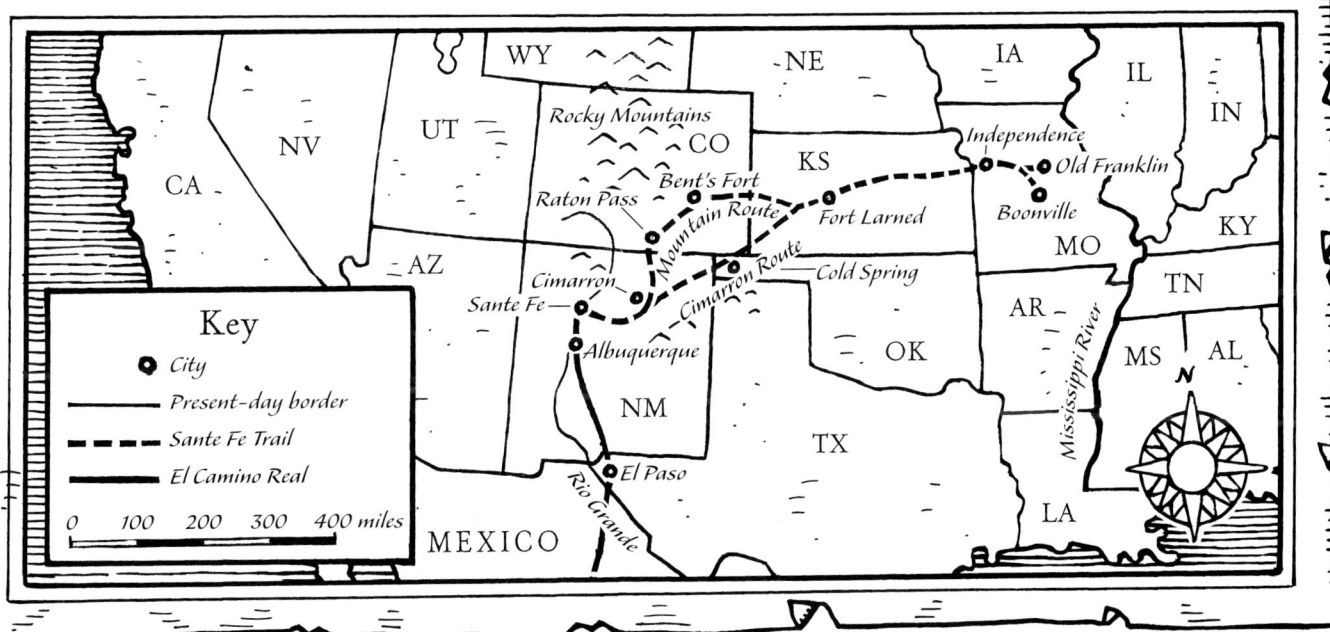

A United States Territory

The Treaty of Guadalupe Hidalgo changed the shape of the United States. Our country's southern boundary, or border, moved farther south along the Rio Grande and the Gila River.

The United States now controlled Texas and land that is in present-day New Mexico, Arizona, California, Nevada, Utah, and parts of Colorado and Wyoming.

The size and shape of the area now known as New Mexico changed again as a result of the **Compromise of 1850**. Before the Compromise of 1850, the United States struggled with how to set

MAP SKILL New Mexico Territory, 1850

Key

- City
- ★ Spanish capital
- — National border
- — State and territory border

▶ New Mexico Territory was much larger than present-day New Mexico.

MAP SKILL Use Map Scale *How many miles long was New Mexico Territory's eastern border?*

boundary lines in the western territories. Slavery issues were also a concern. With boundary issues resolved by the Compromise of 1850, more and more people were moving into the western territories and the New Mexico area. The United States government wanted to maintain order in these new settlements.

When the United States Congress passed the Compromise of 1850, it established the Territory of New Mexico. A **territory** is an area that is not admitted as a state but has its own lawmaking group. The Compromise of 1850 also settled the dispute with Texas over the land east of the Rio Grande. That land was recognized as part of New Mexico. You can see on the map that parts of what is now New Mexico, Arizona, Nevada, and Colorado made up the New Mexico Territory.

▶ This picture shows a meeting of representatives of the United States and of Mexico.

New Mexico's territorial government was different from the government of a state. The United States government appointed the governors and judges in a territory. The people elected representatives to make laws for their territory. In contrast, the people of a state elected most of their state leaders.

Many settlers who came from the United States wanted New Mexico to remain a United States territory. Other New Mexicans wanted statehood. They wanted New Mexico to become a state and elect its own leaders.

You will read in the next lesson how New Mexico continued to change as part of the United States. The size of New Mexico would increase and decrease before its present-day boundaries were established.

REVIEW What was the difference between the territorial government and the government of a state?
Compare and Contrast

Summarize the Lesson

1692 Don Diego de Vargas brought settlers back to New Mexico.

1821 Mexico gained independence and controlled New Mexico.

1850 New Mexico became a territory of the United States.

LESSON 3 REVIEW

Check Facts and Main Ideas

1. Sequence On a separate sheet of paper, copy the chart below. Fill in these events in Santa Fe that affected the Pueblo people's human rights in the correct order: The Pueblo in Santa Fe surrender to de Vargas; Spanish soldiers return and then retreat; Spanish soldiers take Santa Fe by force.

1681

↓

1692

↓

1693

2. As New Mexico's population grew, how did settlements change?

3. What important events affected New Mexico in the 1700s and early 1800s?

4. Choose one of the following events and explain its significance: the start of the Santa Fe Trail; the appointment of Albino Pérez as governor; the Mexican War; the Treaty of Guadalupe Hidalgo.

5. Critical Thinking: *Infer* Why do you think boundaries were important to people living in New Mexico **Territory?**

Link to History

Research a Biography Select one of the people named in this lesson. Use library resources or the Internet to research more about that person's life. Write a brief report about the way that person's activities influenced New Mexico.

Map and Globe Skills

Use a Historical Map

What? A historical map shows information about events, people, or places in the past. It uses symbols, colors, or patterns to show where an event took place or how a place changed. A historical map may show battles, land claims, or routes of exploration. It may also tell you something about people in the past, such as where they lived or migrated.

Why? Historical maps help you learn about history. You will find these kinds of maps in books about history and in atlases. Historical maps also appear in magazines and newspapers to give background information for current events.

Zebulon Pike's Route, 1806–1807

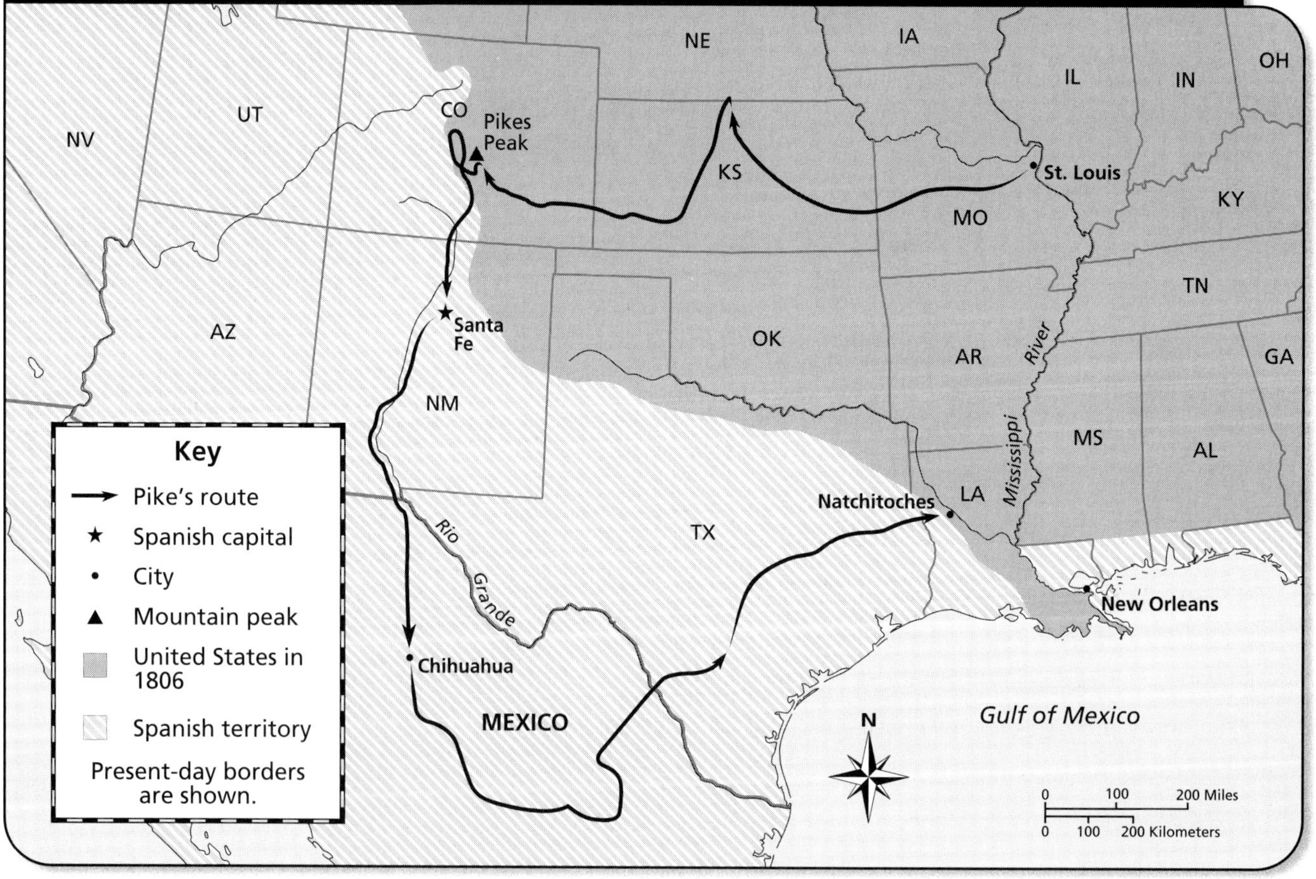

NE IA IL IN OH

UT CO Pikes Peak

NV

KS St. Louis KY

MO

AZ Santa Fe OK TN

NM AR GA

MS AL

Natchitoches LA

TX

Chihuahua New Orleans

MEXICO

N Gulf of Mexico

Key
- → Pike's route
- ★ Spanish capital
- • City
- ▲ Mountain peak
- United States in 1806
- Spanish territory

Present-day borders are shown.

0 100 200 Miles
0 100 200 Kilometers

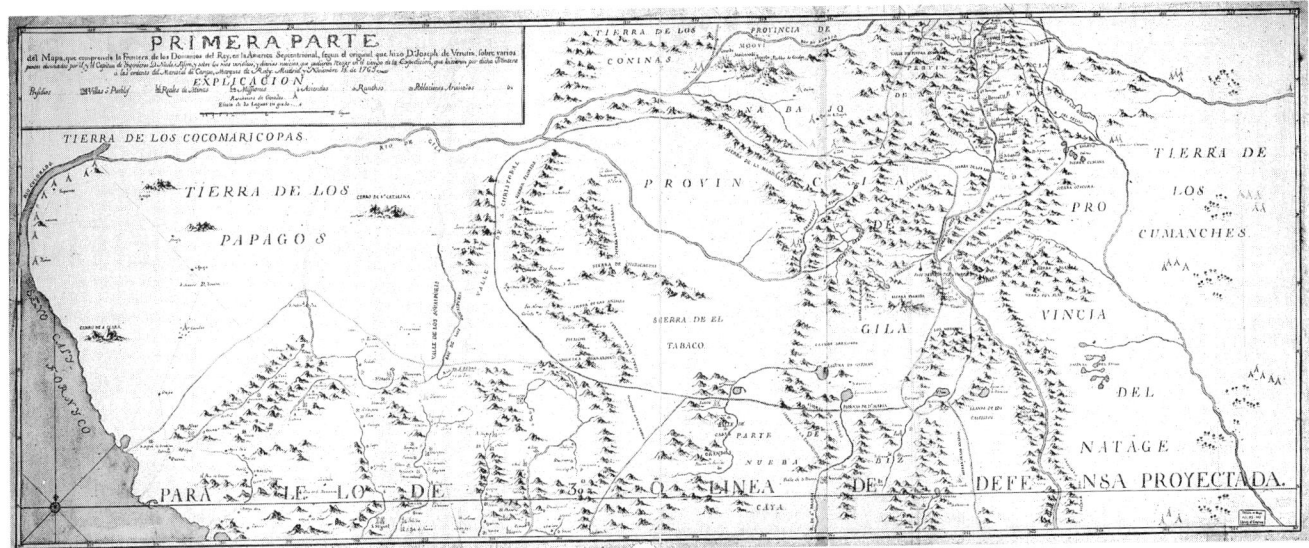

PRIMERA PARTE

▶ **This map of Spanish territory in parts of North America was drawn in 1769. It shows land that is now New Mexico, Arizona, Texas, and northern Mexico.**

On a historical map you can easily see how boundaries or names of places have changed. A historical map can also provide different kinds of information about the past. The historical map on page 72 shows the route taken by Zebulon Pike as he traveled west of the Mississippi River.

The map above is an example of a historical map from long ago. It shows some of the same area as the map on page 72.

How? First, read the title of the map to find out what event or place it shows. Then study the symbols and patterns the map uses to tell about the past. To understand the meaning of these items, you must read the map key. Look at the map on page 72. Read the title and then find the key. What symbols, shades, or patterns does the map use to give information about Zebulon Pike's route? What does each item in the key mean?

The map on page 72 shows that Pike started in St. Louis and traveled through part of the Rocky Mountains. He then continued into New Mexico and Mexico before reaching Louisiana.

Think and Apply

❶ In which direction did Pike travel through New Mexico?

❷ Where did Pike go after he left New Mexico and before he arrived in Texas?

❸ Where did Pike's expedition end?

For more information, go online to the *Atlas* at **www.sfsocialstudies.com.**

LESSON 4

1850   1860   1870   1880

1853
Gadsden
Purchase

1862
Battle of
Glorieta Pass

1878
First railroad arrives
in New Mexico.

Glorieta Pass
Bosque Redondo
Valverde

The Territorial Years

PREVIEW

Focus on the Main Idea
The New Mexico Territory experienced growth and conflict during the 1800s.

PLACES
Valverde
Glorieta Pass
Bosque Redondo

PEOPLE
James Gadsden
Francis Boyer

VOCABULARY
homesteader

EVENTS
Gadsden Purchase
Civil War

▶ Railroads brought change to New Mexico.

You Are There You and your family are in town to buy supplies, and you hear some surprising news. The New Mexico Territory is bigger than it used to be. Last week the United States paid Mexico for some land that has become part of the New Mexico Territory.

On the way home, you think about how you can see Big Hatchet Peak in the distance each morning. That mountain once belonged to Mexico. Now it is part of the New Mexico Territory.

That wasn't all the exciting news you heard. People were talking about a railroad that might be built across that newly purchased land. Your parents tell you that a new railroad could bring more people into the New Mexico Territory. You have never seen a train, but maybe you will before long. You might even get to take a ride on one!

Main Idea and Details As you read, look for details about changes that affected the New Mexico Territory and its people in the late 1800s.

New Boundaries

In Lesson 3 you learned that New Mexico became a United States territory in 1850. As a territory, New Mexico grew to include the area that is now New Mexico, Arizona, and parts of Colorado, Utah, and Nevada.

Soon the size of the New Mexico Territory would change again. In 1853 **James Gadsden,** a United States representative to Mexico, arranged for the United States to buy land from Mexico. In return for $10 million, Mexico sold part of its land to the United States. The **Gadsden Purchase** finally settled the southern boundary of the New Mexico Territory.

The Gadsden Purchase gave the New Mexico Territory new land and new possibilities. Pressure to build a transcontinental railroad was growing. The newly purchased land provided a path for such a project. Tracks could now be laid across flat desert land instead of through mountains. However, it would still be many years before this dream became a reality.

A few years later, the northern boundary of the New Mexico Territory was changed. The discovery of gold in what is now Colorado drew many people to that area. The population grew, and in 1861 the United States government formed the Colorado Territory. The United States Congress decided to use a line of latitude for the border between the Colorado and

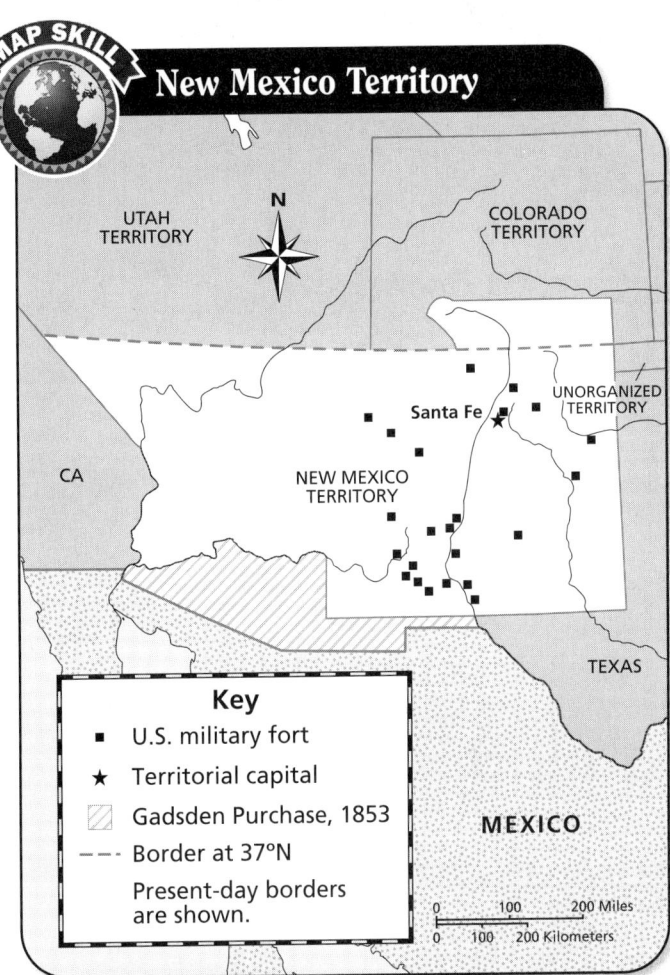

MAP SKILL **New Mexico Territory**

Key
- ■ U.S. military fort
- ★ Territorial capital
- ▨ Gadsden Purchase, 1853
- --- Border at 37°N
- Present-day borders are shown.

▶ **New Mexico's boundaries changed during the 1850s and 1860s. As the population grew, forts were built.**

MAP SKILL Understand Directions *In what direction from Santa Fe did most of the forts lie?*

New Mexico Territories. The map on this page shows the new border at 37°N. It also shows land area lost by the New Mexico Territory to the Colorado Territory.

During the 1850s and 1860s, some Native American groups increased raids on settlements in the New Mexico Territory. The settlers were using land that Native Americans had used for hunting. The map on this page shows the numerous forts built to protect people from these attacks.

REVIEW What effect did the Gadsden Purchase have on the New Mexico Territory? **Cause and Effect**

▶ **Fort Union was built in 1851 to protect people in New Mexico.**

▶ The plaza in Santa Fe was a center of activity, especially for traders and other travelers.

A Young Territory

The decades of the 1850s and 1860s were a time of expansion and growth in New Mexico. The Santa Fe Trail provided a route to Santa Fe and the territory. Protection provided by the forts made settlers in the area feel safer. Conflict with Native American groups became less common. As a result, people became more interested in settling in the New Mexico Territory.

During this time, many merchants, farmers, and prospectors came westward. Many people were on their way to California. There they hoped to find gold. Along the way, many people passed through the New Mexico Territory. Some of them decided to settle here. People were excited about making a new life in this growing territory.

Many other factors led to the growth of the New Mexico Territory as well. One such factor involved new and expanded systems of travel. For example, the first cross-country stagecoach ran through the area in 1858. A stagecoach is a horse-drawn vehicle. This and other forms of transportation encouraged settlement.

The New Mexico Territory offered people many opportunities. The mountains and hills drew miners who looked for minerals such as silver, gold, and copper. Sheep and cattle ranchers searched out the most fertile pastureland.

Ranchers in New Mexico included native New Mexicans and Texans. During the 1860s ranchers drove their herds of cattle up the Pecos River. The Native American reservations and mining towns were ideal markets for the ranchers' beef. A reservation is land that the United States government sets aside for Native Americans to live on.

The Homestead Act was passed by the United States Congress in 1862. Some settlers in the New Mexico Territory became homesteaders. A **homesteader** is a settler granted land by the United States government. A small fee allowed a homesteader to claim 160 acres. To keep the land, a homesteader needed to build a home on it and farm the land for five years.

The Homestead Act drew American settlers to the area with the promise of cheap land. Settlers came to the New Mexico Territory to build homes, farms, and ranches. Many homesteaders built small log cabins on their farms in the hope of starting a better life.

Even as people came looking for opportunities, there were hard times in the New Mexico Territory. Next you will read about how war affected the territory.

REVIEW What contributed to New Mexico's growth in the 1850s?

⊙ **Summarize**

Transportation Changes

Then and Now

Stagecoaches began carrying passengers to New Mexico on the Santa Fe Trail in 1849. In 1858 John Butterfield used stagecoaches for his Butterfield Overland Mail service from St. Louis to San Francisco. As railroads were built, train service gradually replaced the stagecoach lines. Today airlines provide transportation to New Mexicans and visitors to our state.

▶ Today thousands of passengers from around the country and the world fly in and out of Albuquerque International Airport.

▶ In the late 1800s, stagecoaches transported passengers and supplies to and from New Mexico.

Conflict in the Territory

In 1861 fighting broke out between Union and Confederate forces in the United States. Union forces were loyal to the U.S. government. Confederate states in the south had broken away from the United States. This marked the beginning of the Civil War. A civil war is a war between groups of people who are citizens of the same country.

One of the issues on which the two sides disagreed was whether slavery should expand to western territories such as New Mexico. Some in the New Mexico Territory supported slavery, but others did not.

Although the New Mexico Territory was far away from the main Civil War battlefields, New Mexicans served as soldiers in the Union forces. Union and Confederate forces battled for control of the New Mexico Territory. Early in the war, Confederate troops captured Fort Fillmore. In 1862 Union forces retreated from Albuquerque and Santa Fe.

That same year, two Civil War battles were fought in the New Mexico Territory. The first occurred in February at Valverde, near Fort Craig in the southern part of the territory. Confederate troops defeated Union forces, which retreated to the fort for safety. In late March Union troops won a key battle at Glorieta Pass (gloh ree ET uh PAS). This Union victory drove Confederate forces out of the New Mexico Territory.

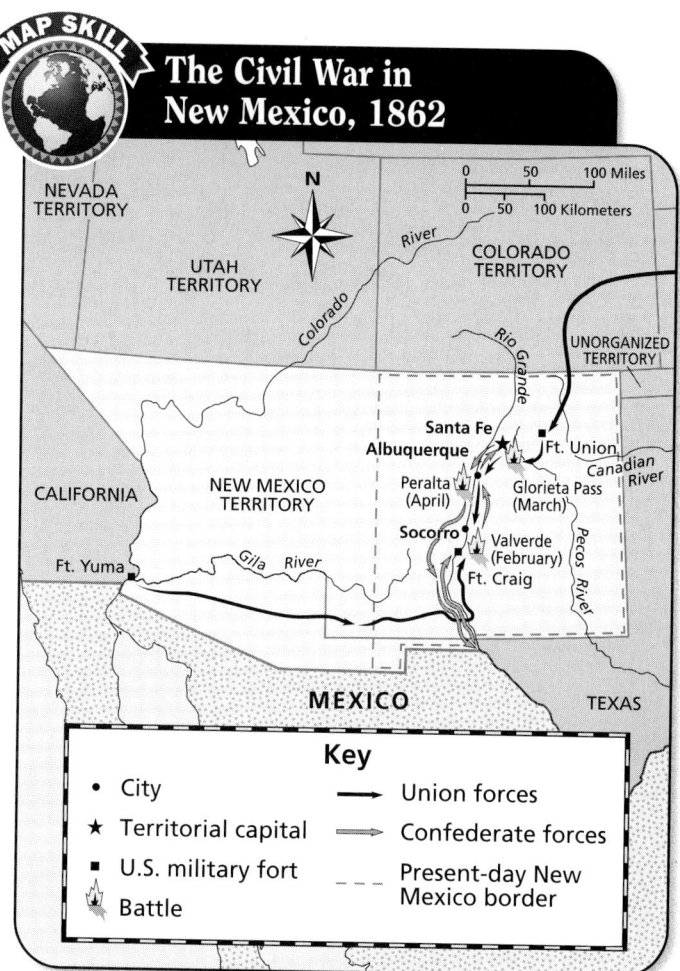

MAP SKILL
The Civil War in New Mexico, 1862

▶ Several Civil War battles occurred along the Rio Grande.

MAP SKILL Trace Movement on Maps
When Union forces traveled through the New Mexico Territory, where did they last stop?

▶ This picture shows the battle that took place at Apache Canyon, just west of Glorieta Pass, on March 26, 1862. Confederate forces retreated. Two days later, Union forces won the Battle of Glorieta Pass.

▶ Members of the Tenth Cavalry were known as "Buffalo Soldiers." Their symbol (above right) features a buffalo.

The boundaries of the New Mexico Territory again changed in 1863, when the United States divided the New Mexico Territory in half. The western portion became the Arizona Territory, and the eastern part remained the New Mexico Territory.

The Civil War ended in 1865. Then in 1898 New Mexicans served in another conflict, the Spanish-American War. The United States opposed Spanish rule in Cuba, a large island south of Florida. The United States sent troops to help the Cuban people fight for independence. New Mexico sent many men to join the U.S. Army. Spain was eventually defeated, and Cuba became independent. Some saw this war as a way for New Mexico to prove its loyalty to the United States. New Mexicans hoped that their support would earn them statehood.

The late 1800s were also filled with conflict between United States troops and Native Americans. The United States military eventually defeated the Diné and sent them to a reservation far from their homeland. This journey to Bosque Redondo (BOHS kay ray DOHN doh) is known as the "long walk." The Apache also were sent to Bosque Redondo. Later United States troops also defeated the Ute and the Comanche.

Troops patrolled much of the New Mexico Territory to keep the peace between settlers and Native Americans. Some of these troops included African Americans. Native Americans called these troops "Buffalo Soldiers" as a sign of respect. It is believed that Native Americans saw the same strength and courage of the buffalo in the African American soldiers. By the late 1880s, all of the Native American groups in New Mexico had been moved to reservations.

An African American named Francis Boyer came to New Mexico in the late 1890s to escape racial violence. He and his wife, Ella, led about 300 African American settlers from Georgia to New Mexico. They founded the town of Blackdom. People lived in Blackdom through the mid-1920s before moving on to other parts of New Mexico.

REVIEW Why was the Battle at Glorieta Pass important? **Main Idea and Details**

79

Railroads and Growth

As railroad lines spread throughout the New Mexico Territory, more settlements grew. The Atchison, Topeka, and Santa Fe was the first railroad to enter the New Mexico Territory. On December 7, 1878, "Uncle Avery" Turner steered the first steam train into the territory. This railroad followed the old path of the Santa Fe Trail. It ran all the way to Albuquerque, where it branched off in different directions.

The Atchison, Topeka, and Santa Fe Railroad later joined the Southern Pacific Railroad, which began in California. These two railroads formed a route that stretched across the country. As you read on page 75, land gained in the Gadsden Purchase helped make this route possible. You can see the railway lines in New Mexico on the map on this page.

Railroads helped turn ranching in the New Mexico Territory into a booming industry in the late 1800s. Railroads could transport New Mexico beef quickly across the country to large eastern cities. Since before the Civil War, U.S. cattle and beef industries began migrating from the east to open land in the west.

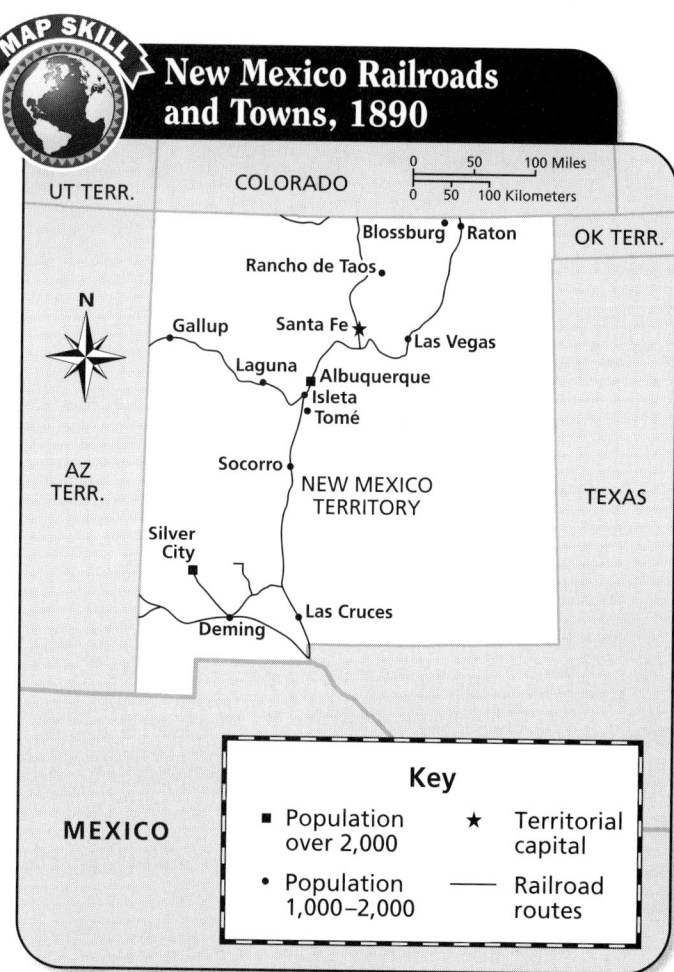

MAP SKILL — New Mexico Railroads and Towns, 1890

Key
- ■ Population over 2,000
- • Population 1,000–2,000
- ★ Territorial capital
- — Railroad routes

▶ Railroads connected many towns in New Mexico in the late 1800s.

MAP SKILL Use Routes *Which towns would a train pass through on the way from Santa Fe to Las Cruces?*

▶ Steam locomotives such as this one in Engle, New Mexico, pulled train cars on the railroad lines. Burning coal, oil, or wood heated water to make the steam, and energy from steam turned the huge wheels.

Easterners grew to depend on western ranchers for their cattle and beef needs. Western ranchers worked to keep up with the increased demand for beef.

In the late 1800s, deposits of silver and gold were found in the New Mexico Territory. Railroads carried people who wanted to work in the mines. Towns and businesses sprang up quickly around the mines. By the early 1900s, most of these minerals had been mined. When the mines closed, people left the towns.

In addition to encouraging growth in ranching and mining, the railroads helped the territory grow in other ways. A new stop on the railroad line often meant that a new town was born. Some towns began as places for repairing and supplying the railroad. New lines were built to many parts of the state. This made it possible for people to settle in new places. Shops and businesses opened to provide them with needed goods.

During the 1900s transportation in New Mexico changed again. Railway lines that were not making a profit were abandoned. Highways were later built alongside the railroad lines, and more and more people traveled by car. You will read about these changes in the next lesson.

REVIEW What effect did railroads have over time on towns and businesses in the New Mexico Territory? **Cause and Effect**

Summarize the Lesson

1853 The Gadsden Purchase increased the size of the New Mexico Territory.

1862 Union forces defeated Confederate forces at the Battle of Glorieta Pass.

1878 The Atchison, Topeka, and Santa Fe Railroad was the first railroad to arrive in New Mexico.

LESSON 4 REVIEW

Check Facts and Main Ideas

1. **Main Idea and Details** On a separate sheet of paper, fill in the chart with details that support the main idea.

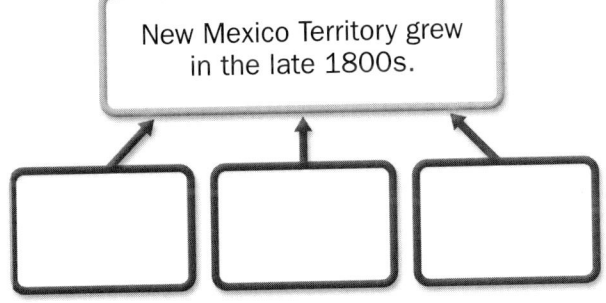

New Mexico Territory grew in the late 1800s.

2. What important events affected the New Mexico Territory during the 1850s and 1860s?
3. Name two Civil War battles fought in the New Mexico Territory. What were the results?
4. Who was Francis Boyer? Why is he important to New Mexico history?
5. **Critical Thinking:** *Categorize* Group homesteaders and others who came to New Mexico in the 1800s by the natural resources they used, such as land or minerals.

Link to **Writing**

Write a Diary Entry Suppose that you have just taken your first trip on the Atchison, Topeka, and Santa Fe Railroad. Write a diary entry describing your trip.

1912
New Mexico gains statehood.

1922
Soledad Chacon is elected to state office.

1945
Atomic bomb is tested at Trinity Site

Los Alamos • • Taos

■ *Trinity Site*

Columbus

PREVIEW

Focus on the Main Idea
During the twentieth century, New Mexico's economy and culture grew.

PLACES
Columbus
Taos
Los Alamos
Trinity Site

PEOPLE
William C. McDonald
Adelina Otero-Warren
Soledad Chacon
Isabel Eckles
D. H. Lawrence
Georgia O'Keeffe
Maria Martinez
Dennis Chavez

VOCABULARY
ally

EVENTS
World War I
Great Depression
World War II

▶ The image on our state flag is the ancient sun symbol of the Zia Pueblo people.

Into the Twentieth Century

You Are There
You wake up early, too excited to sleep. You dress quickly. You finish your sign that says "The STATE of New Mexico." Today the New Mexico Territory gains its statehood.

Later, you and your family walk to the plaza. Today no one is working. A band is playing songs. Homes and businesses are decorated with flags. You proudly hold your sign and wait.

Finally, you hear the official announcement. The President of the United States has signed a special document. It announces that New Mexico is a state. As the parade begins, you wave your sign and join the chorus of cheers. Hurray for statehood!

Cause and Effect As you read, think about how the constitutional convention in New Mexico affected the structure of the state government.

A New State

As a United States territory, New Mexico enjoyed certain benefits. However, many New Mexicans came to believe that statehood might better benefit New Mexico. Others did not support statehood. They thought that they might have to pay too many taxes.

Many people in other parts of the United States were not familiar with New Mexico. Some members of the United States Congress wondered whether New Mexico's population would be loyal. They felt that New Mexico's past as part of Mexico might mean that some citizens were loyal to Mexico. However, many New Mexicans believed that they had already proved their loyalty to the United States. For example, many New Mexicans had fought for the Union during the Civil War.

Finally, in 1910, New Mexico held a constitutional convention. Representatives here wrote a constitution and designed the structure of state government. It would have executive, legislative, and judicial branches. Most citizens would be able to elect their state leaders. At this time, most Native Americans could not vote. However, many of New Mexico's Native American groups would later be able to elect their own tribal councils.

On January 6, 1912, the U.S. Congress accepted New Mexico's constitution, and New Mexico became our nation's forty-seventh state. Soon after this event, William C. McDonald became the first governor of the state of New Mexico.

REVIEW Why did some New Mexicans believe that New Mexico should become a state? **Main Idea and Details**

▶ Representatives to the constitutional convention met in Santa Fe in 1910. Voters approved the constitution the following year.

▶ William C. McDonald, a rancher from Carrizozo, became the state's first governor in 1912.

World War I

In 1914, two years after New Mexico became a state, World War I broke out in Europe. Great Britain, France, Russia, Italy, and Japan formed the Allied Powers. An ally is a person, group, or nation united with another for some special purpose. The Allied Powers fought against the Central Powers of Germany, Austria-Hungary, and the Ottoman Empire. At first the United States did not enter the war. However, the United States faced a different challenge.

In Mexico, Pancho Villa (PAHN choh VEE yah) was a rebel leader, or someone who fights against the government in power. Villa fought against Mexican forces during the Mexican Revolution. He wanted to show that he controlled northern Mexico. He raided Columbus in New Mexico. This town lies near Mexico's northern border.

Merchants in Columbus had not delivered weapons that Villa had paid for. People on both sides died. United States soldiers fought back, but Villa escaped. Then the United States sent General John Pershing with additional troops to New Mexico to prevent more attacks. Pershing's forces spent 11 months searching for Villa, but they never found him.

Pershing's forces left New Mexico in 1917. Later that year the United States entered World War I on the side of the Allies. Pershing was sent to Europe, where he commanded United States forces.

People in New Mexico supported the war effort in a number of ways. Our state became a training area for United States troops. Thousands of New Mexicans served their country. Some became soldiers, and others helped at home.

▶ New Mexican troops gained combat experience in the conflict with Pancho Villa. Supply trains were organized at this army camp at Columbus. Many of these soldiers later fought in Europe during World War I.

▶ Copper from mines such as this one in New Mexico contributed to the war effort.

Groups throughout New Mexico organized to work for the war effort. At this time New Mexico was mainly an agricultural state, so farmers planted more food crops. Women worked in agriculture or in the few factories that existed. Doctors developed new ways to care for injured soldiers.

The state's mining industry also contributed to the war effort. Many kinds of war supplies needed to be manufactured, including tanks, planes, trucks, and communication equipment. All of these products required metal, especially copper. New Mexico's mines provided much of the supply.

In the years before the war, mining production had slowed in New Mexico. However, during the war some mines set new records for copper production.

Change once again came to the country and to New Mexico after World War I. The Central Powers surrendered in 1918, and a treaty was signed in 1919. Women had contributed much during the war, and opportunities for women continued to grow. In 1920 women in the United States gained the right to vote. They could also run for political office. Women in New Mexico took advantage of these new rights. From 1917 to 1929 Adelina "Nina" Otero-Warren (ah de LEE nuh NEE nuh oh TAIR oh WOR

en) was a government worker. She worked to help New Mexico's schools and to organize help for Native Americans. In 1922 Soledad Chacon (soh le DAHD chah KOHN) and Isabel Eckles became the first New Mexican women elected to statewide offices.

REVIEW What happened as a result of Pancho Villa's raid on Columbus, New Mexico? ⟳ Summarize

▶ Soledad Chacon was elected secretary of state of New Mexico in 1922.

85

Between the Wars

The 1920s and 1930s were years of change for the country. It was no different in New Mexico. Events during this time affected our country's economy. At the same time, artists in our state became widely known and influenced culture.

In the early 1900s, many people across the country were drawn to our state because of its climate and natural beauty. During this time many well-known writers and painters moved to New Mexico. **D. H. Lawrence,** a British writer, lived in **Taos** for a while during the 1920s. He wrote novels, short stories, and poems. He was greatly influenced by the natural beauty of New Mexico. You can read what he said about living here on page 1.

By the early 1930s, many artists also lived in New Mexico. **Georgia O'Keeffe** was one of the best-known painters in the United States. In 1929 she began spending summers in New Mexico. Much of her art features elements of New Mexico's landscape.

Pottery was another art form practiced in New Mexico. One influential potter was **Maria Martinez.** She created a unique type of pottery. You will read more about her in the Biography feature on page 92.

As they had done for centuries, Native Americans also created art and handcrafted items. They designed jewelry made of turquoise and silver. During this period Native American arts and crafts became well known throughout the state and across the country.

Two towns in New Mexico became centers for artists and their art. Artists living in Taos formed a group that helped make people aware of New Mexico's art. People in Santa Fe influenced architecture. Many of the buildings in the city were built in the Pueblo style. These buildings are similar in color and shape to the buildings in traditional Pueblo communities. This style of building gradually became popular in other parts of our country.

▶ Maria Martinez helped develop greater awareness of Native American arts and crafts.

▶ D. H. Lawrence lived on a ranch near Taos. Today the ranch is a center for arts education.

▶ Georgia O'Keeffe was famous for her paintings of flowers and bones.

▶ The Dust Bowl extended into New Mexico's Great Plains region. The dry soil was kicked up by winds, and dust clouds darkened the sky.

While art flourished in New Mexico, economic changes swept the nation. In 1929 the United States entered a period called the **Great Depression.** It lasted throughout the 1930s. A depression is a period when businesses are not very active and many people do not have jobs. During a depression fewer goods are produced. Workers lose their jobs because companies cannot afford to pay them. The Great Depression was a very severe depression that lasted for many years.

Other events in the 1930s also presented challenges. During this time a series of droughts struck the Midwest. Huge dust storms such as the one pictured above rolled across the Great Plains. The area they covered became known as the Dust Bowl. These dust storms reached eastern New Mexico, causing hardships for farmers and ranchers.

President Franklin D. Roosevelt worked with Congress to help the country recover from the Great Depression. New government programs helped farmers

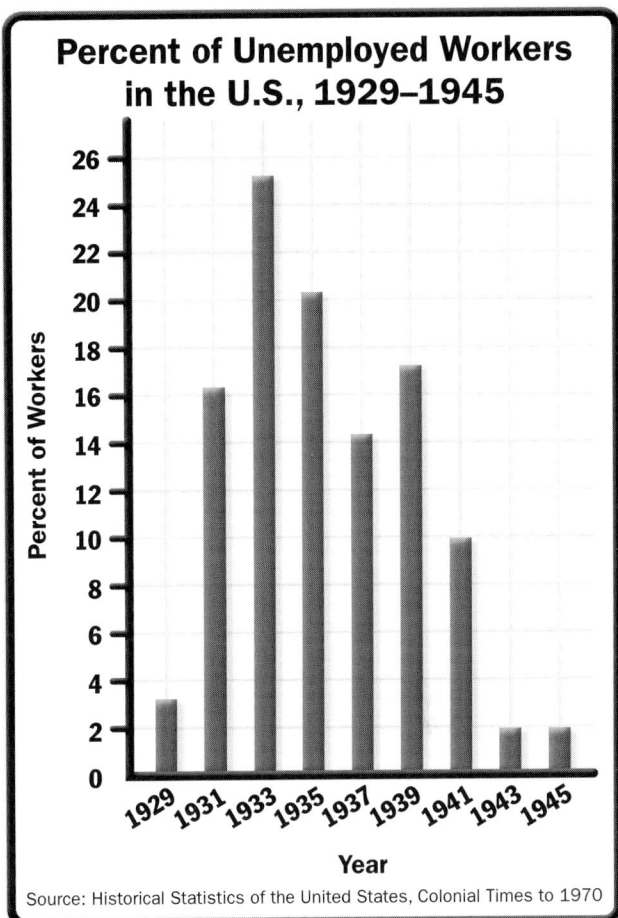

Percent of Unemployed Workers in the U.S., 1929–1945

Source: Historical Statistics of the United States, Colonial Times to 1970

▶ Unemployment rose greatly between 1929 and 1931.

GRAPH SKILL *According to the graph, during which year was the highest percentage of workers unemployed?*

by supporting prices for farm goods. Government projects gave workers jobs, such as building dams in New Mexico. Some programs helped Native Americans on reservations.

New Mexico's U.S. senator at the time, **Dennis Chavez** (DEN is CHAH vez), supported these government programs. You will read more about Chavez in the Citizen Heroes feature on page 93.

REVIEW What events during the 1930s affected New Mexico and the nation?
Main Idea and Details

World War II

During the 1930s another war broke out overseas. **World War II** began in Europe in 1939. At first the United States stayed out of the war. However, on December 7, 1941, Japanese planes bombed the United States naval base at Pearl Harbor, Hawaii. The United States then entered the war. It fought on the side of Great Britain, France, and the former Soviet Union against Japan, Germany, and Italy.

New Mexico's soldiers played a role in the war. Thousands of New Mexicans served in the military. Two New Mexico regiments fought at the battle of Bataan (beh TAN) in the Philippines. When Bataan fell to Japanese forces, the captured Allied soldiers were forced to march for days to prison camps. The soldiers from New Mexico later were honored for their bravery.

▶ Each year thousands of people from New Mexico and other states who served in the military take part in the Bataan Memorial Death March at White Sands Missile Base. It honors those who served in the Philippine Islands during World War II.

NEW MEXICO
BUY   BUY
COMPRE COMPRE COMPRE
AWONG-GEEH ACOO-MAN DA-AH
WAR
BONDS AND STAMPS

▶ During World War II, some posters in New Mexico included messages in English, Spanish, and Native American languages.

One of New Mexico's most famous soldiers was cartoonist Bill Mauldin. Mauldin served in the army. He drew cartoons about the everyday lives of soldiers. His cartoons were seen in hundreds of newspapers across the country. Mauldin's cartoons won major prizes.

During World War II, many women served as nurses and worked close to enemy lines. Others joined the U.S. Army, Navy, Marines, and Coast Guard, where they performed valuable services. A special group of women pilots in the Army Air Corps flew planes within the United States. This allowed men to fly planes for the war effort.

New Mexicans also helped the war effort at home. As in World War I, war industries needed our state's rich mineral deposits. Copper, zinc, tin, and other minerals from New Mexico's mines helped produce airplanes, tanks, and ships.

One of the most significant events of World War II occurred in New Mexico. In 1943 the United States government built a secret science laboratory in northern New Mexico near Santa Fe. A team of scientists worked to develop an atomic bomb. The government built the town of **Los Alamos** (lohs AL uh mohs) around the laboratory. The scientists and their families lived in Los Alamos. The atomic bomb project was kept secret. During the war no one except the scientists and their families were allowed into Los Alamos.

In July 1945, scientists tested the atomic bomb at a place called **Trinity Site** in the White Sands area near Alamogordo. The test was a success. The United States now had the most powerful weapon ever known. The Allies already had defeated Germany in May 1945, but Japan continued to battle. In August 1945, United States planes dropped two atomic bombs on the Japanese cities of Hiroshima and Nagasaki. Many thousands of people died. Soon the Japanese surrendered and the war ended.

After World War II, scientists remained at the Los Alamos Laboratory. It continues to be an important center for scientific research.

REVIEW What effect did the atomic bombs have on World War II?
Cause and Effect

▶ Pictured on the left is one of the scientists who developed the atomic bomb. He is standing at Trinity Site after the bomb was tested.

▶ When the atomic bomb was first tested, observers said that the explosion lit the sky more brightly than the sun does.

New Mexico After World War II

After the end of World War II, people turned their attention to life at home. Soon life in New Mexico and throughout the country began to change.

New Mexico's population grew rapidly after World War II. Many people started families. Other people moved to our state from other places.

As you can see on the graph, New Mexico's cities were also growing. For years, many New Mexicans had lived in rural areas. After World War II, people began moving from rural areas to the cities. They wanted to find jobs in manufacturing, oil and gas production, and scientific research.

New types of mining became key to New Mexico's economy. In the 1950s mining for uranium and potash began in New Mexico. Scientists need uranium to produce atomic energy and manufacture weapons. Potash is a key ingredient in fertilizer. New Mexico produces more potash than any other state.

New Mexico also experienced growth in industries. Today electronic instruments

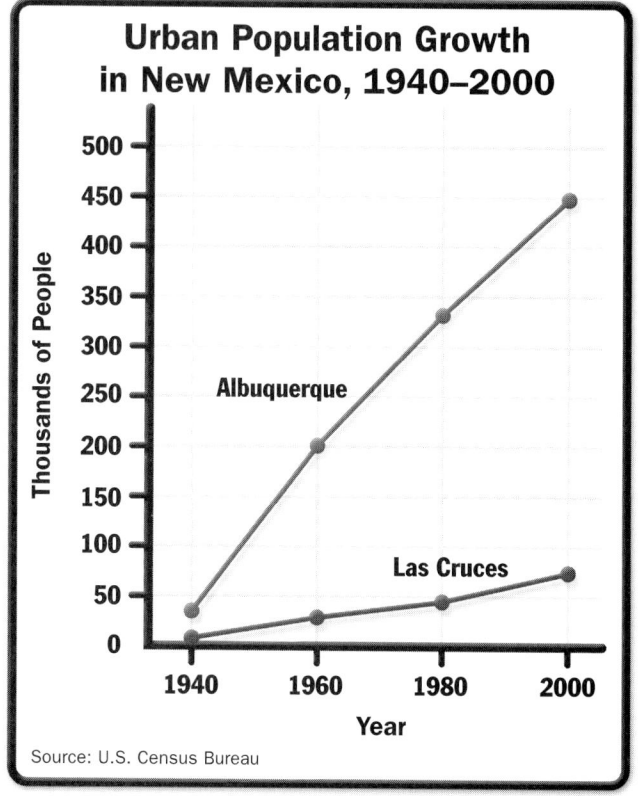

Urban Population Growth in New Mexico, 1940–2000

Albuquerque

Las Cruces

Source: U.S. Census Bureau

▶ Albuquerque has grown much faster than other cities in New Mexico.

GRAPH SKILL *According to the graph, what was the population of Albuquerque in 1960?*

and military defense systems form much of our state's manufacturing.

In the last half of the twentieth century, tourism became a leading industry in New Mexico. Roads were improved and air transportation increased. It became easier for people to travel to our state.

▶ This uranium mill near Grants opened in 1959. At that time it was able to process about 3,600 tons of uranium per day.

Our state's natural beauty, historic sites, and varied cultures draw people from across the country and around the world. In the next chapter you will learn more about New Mexico today.

REVIEW Name two industries that grew in New Mexico after World War II.
Main Idea and Details

Summarize the Lesson

1912 New Mexico became the forty-seventh state.

1922 Soledad Chacon was the first New Mexican woman elected to state office.

1945 An atomic bomb was tested at Trinity Site near Alamogordo.

▶ **A huge balloon festival in Albuquerque attracts many visitors to New Mexico.**

LESSON 5 REVIEW

Check Facts and Main Ideas

1. **Cause and Effect** On a separate sheet of paper, fill in the effects of the constitutional convention on the structure of state government.

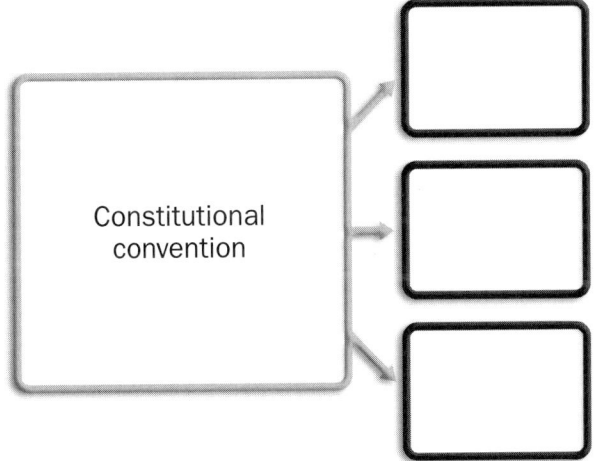

Constitutional convention

2. How did New Mexicans contribute to the war efforts of the United States and its **allies** during World War I?

3. How did the artists who lived in New Mexico in the early 1900s influence culture?

4. What was the importance of the laboratory at Los Alamos?

5. **Critical Thinking: Predict** Which type of economic activity do you think will grow the most in the next 50 years? Why?

Link to Science

Scientific Discoveries Use materials from your school or local library to find out more about the discoveries made at Los Alamos since World War II. Share the information you find with the class.

Maria Martinez

1880s?–1980

Watch and learn. Then teach others. Maria Martinez was a successful Pueblo potter who made good use of these simple instructions. Usually Pueblo girls learn pottery making from their mothers, grandmothers, or aunts.

When she was about eleven years old, Maria watched her aunt make pottery at the San Ildefonso pueblo. Most people at San Ildefonso had stopped making pottery by the 1800s. Today San Ildefonso is known for its pottery.

Maria attended school, but she had no formal training in pottery. In 1904 she married Julian Martinez. In the early 1920s, the couple developed an original style of "black-on-black" pottery. This pottery featured dull black designs on a polished black background.

BIOFACT

Martinez did not use a potter's wheel to shape the clay. Instead, she rolled long ribbons of clay, formed each into a circle, and stacked the circles. Then she rubbed all the clay until the piece was perfectly smooth.

Martinez taught others at San Ildefonso how to make black-on-black pottery. Making pottery brought employment opportunities to the pueblo.

"We don't care about being well known or anything. Pueblo Indian people don't think about things like that. We all just want to get along in this world and be together."

Learn from Biographies

How did Maria Martinez's talent as a potter help the people of San Ildefonso pueblo keep a tradition alive?

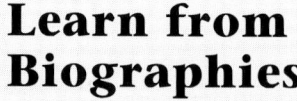 Students can research the lives of significant people by clicking on *Meet the People* at **www.sfsocialstudies.com**.

CITIZEN HEROES

BUILDING CITIZENSHIP
Caring
Respect
Responsibility
⭐ **Fairness**
Honesty
Courage

Working for Justice

How can we make sure that people are treated fairly? Read how Dennis Chavez worked to protect the rights of people of different cultures and backgrounds.

Dennis Chavez grew up helping others. Born in 1888, he grew up in Los Chavez and Albuquerque. He left school at age thirteen to work in a grocery store to help his family. However, Chavez continued reading books about history and political leaders. Chavez decided to help others through politics.

Chavez was elected to New Mexico's House of Representatives in 1922. From 1931 to 1935, he served in the United States House of Representatives. Chavez served as a United States senator from 1935 until his death in 1962.

Throughout his career Chavez worked to protect human rights. He fought for laws that provided fair treatment for workers. He defended civil rights for all New Mexicans. Chavez also helped develop New Mexico's economy.

A statue of Chavez stands in the United States Capitol in Washington, D.C. These words are written in Spanish on the statue:

> *"This man left behind a path that would never be forgotten. He did this in the hope that others would follow."*

Chavez set an example of working for fairness that others can follow.

Fairness in Action

Link to Current Events What are some examples of how people in your community protect the rights of others?

Chapter Summary

 **Summarize**

On a separate sheet of paper, copy the chart below. Fill in details that support the summary statement.

> Three Native American groups lived in what is now New Mexico when the Spanish arrived.

Main Ideas and Skills

1 New Mexico's early people belonged to which two groups?

2 How did Pueblo peoples and early Spanish settlers make sure that they would have water?

3 **Main Idea** How did Mexican control affect trade in New Mexico?

4 **Main Idea** How did the boundaries of the New Mexico Territory change in the mid-1800s?

5 **Critical Thinking:** *Categorize* What kinds of contributions did New Mexico make to our nation in the twentieth century?

Apply Skills

Use a Historical Map Study the map on page 72. Then answer the question.

6 According to the map, what Mexican town did Zebulon Pike visit?

Vocabulary, People, and Terms

Match each word with the correct definition.

1 archaeologist (p. 47)

2 expedition (p. 55)

3 migrate (p. 58)

4 homesteader (p. 77)

5 ally (p. 84)

a. a long and carefully organized trip

b. settler granted land by the U.S. government

c. person, group, or nation united with another for some special purpose

d. person who studies people, customs, and life of ancient times

e. to move from one place in order to settle in another

Write a sentence about each of the following people or terms. You may use two or more in a single sentence.

6 hunter-gatherer (p. 48)

7 Don Juan de Oñate (p. 58)

8 land grant (p. 64)

9 James Gadsden (p. 75)

10 Maria Martinez (pp. 86, 92)

Write About History

1 **Write a journal entry** describing your life and work in a Spanish settlement in New Mexico during the 1700s.

2 **Write a speech** that explains why you think the New Mexico Territory should or should not become a state.

3 **Write a letter** to a friend describing artists you learned about during a visit to Taos and Santa Fe during the early 1900s.

New Mexico Today

CHAPTER 3

Lesson 1

Albuquerque

Albuquerque's city government provides services and protection for its people.

Lesson 2

Santa Fe

Santa Fe is the oldest capital city in the United States.

Lesson 3

Fort Sumner

New Mexico's economy depends on resources, including wind energy found near Fort Sumner.

Lesson 4

Columbus

Columbus is an important trade and transportation center on the United States–Mexico border.

Lesson 5

Socorro

Scientists in Socorro operate one of the world's largest radio telescopes.

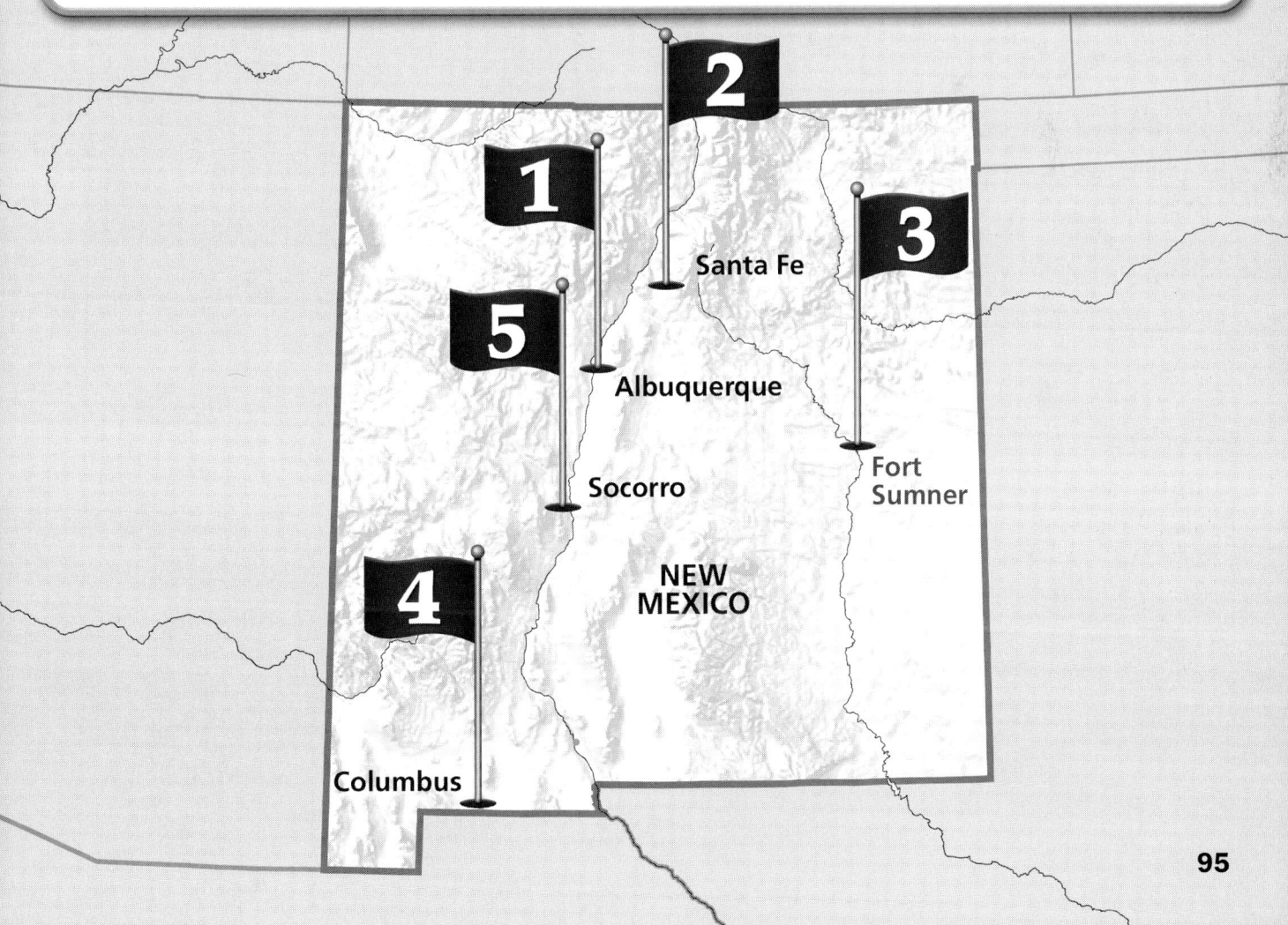

PREVIEW

Focus on the Main Idea
A government serves its people, who have both rights and responsibilities.

PLACES
Albuquerque
Cochiti Lake

VOCABULARY
resident
right
responsibility
citizenship

TERM
community college

▶ Fire engines have many special features, such as a toolbox and a water tanker, that are necessary for fighting fires.

Government and Citizenship

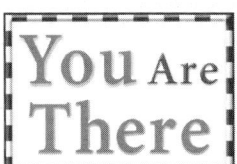 Today your uncle is taking you to the fire station where he works. When you arrive, you see firefighters sweeping floors and washing dishes. You are surprised, but your uncle explains. "Life at the fire station isn't always exciting," he says.

Other firefighters are washing the fire engine. Your uncle lets you climb up and sit behind the steering wheel. He explains some of the controls. When the crew finishes, they go inside to clean up and cook dinner.

While you and your uncle set the table, the firefighters share stories of some of the fires they have battled. Just then the fire alarm sounds. The firefighters spring into action. Within minutes you see the red blur of the fire engine and hear its siren scream as it races to battle another fire.

 **Summarize** As you read, summarize how New Mexicans fulfill their responsibilities and practice good citizenship.

How Government Serves the People

Fire protection is only one of many services that governments in New Mexico provide. The governments of most cities and towns provide basic services to residents. A **resident** is a person living in a place. Basic services can include collecting garbage and supplying water.

New Mexico's state and local governments also provide transportation services. They may build and repair streets and roads. This makes it possible for people and goods to move from place to place. The cities of **Albuquerque,** Las Cruces, and Santa Fe operate buses that transport people. Perhaps you have taken a bus in one of these cities.

Government also offers educational opportunities to all New Mexicans. About 750 public schools are located throughout our state. In addition, New Mexico has many community colleges and public universities. A **community college** is a school that offers the first two years of college courses.

▶ Two major highways meet in Albuquerque. State and national government money paid for improvements to make the highways safer for drivers.

Local and state governments operate places where people can enjoy themselves. These include parks, community centers, golf courses, and sports fields. Local and state governments also provide police to enforce the laws and protect people. Like firefighters, police officers work to make New Mexico a safe place in which to live.

REVIEW Name four services that government in New Mexico provides.
Main Idea and Details

▶ Fire departments are one of the services provided by government. This firefighter in Alamogordo is checking to make sure a house fire is completely out.

Why We Have Rules and Laws

How would your school be different if it did not have rules? Suppose that students could talk whenever they wanted. What if students could come and go from their classrooms as they pleased? How might these actions make learning difficult?

These examples show why your school has rules. Rules help keep order in the school. They also protect the safety and property of you, your classmates, and your teachers.

Now think about the state of New Mexico. You know that almost 2 million people live here. What might happen if everyone could do what they wanted when they wanted? What difficulties might that cause?

Much like your school, the state of New Mexico and your local governments also have rules. These rules are known as laws. Laws are rules that everyone must obey. Laws help keep peace and order throughout New Mexico. Although you may not realize it, these laws affect you daily.

In Chapter 1 you read about the importance of water in New Mexico. State laws ensure that this important resource is shared in an orderly manner. City laws also help control water use. For instance, Farmington does not allow residents to water their lawns during water shortages.

▶ **Students follow rules in class such as raising their hands for permission to speak. In this way students can talk about what they are learning and hear what others say. Rules help make school a good place to learn.**

Traffic laws also help keep order in New Mexico. City and state laws set speed limits for roads and highways. Drivers must follow the laws for traffic lights and stop signs. Criminal laws help prevent harm to people and their possessions. Stealing is an example of an act that breaks a criminal law.

In addition to maintaining peace and order, laws also help protect the safety of New Mexicans. For example, the roads outside your school may have reduced speed limits. State law requires drivers to slow down when passing a school. This law protects students crossing the street to get to or from school. Another state law requires all vehicles to stop while students are getting on or off nearby school buses.

Other laws require that New Mexicans take actions to protect themselves. For example, a state law says that all people in the front seat of a car or truck must wear a seatbelt. If you live in Los Alamos County, you must wear a helmet when you ride a bicycle if you are age 18 or younger.

As you can see, many rules and laws contribute to the public well-being in New Mexico. This means that they work to the benefit or advantage of the state's people.

REVIEW Why do we have laws in New Mexico? **Main Idea and Details**

▶ A police officer explains the laws that must be followed when riding a bicycle. Wearing a helmet when riding a bike can prevent injuries if you have an accident.

▶ Freedom of religion guarantees people the right to their religious beliefs. New Mexicans are free to follow Islam, Judaism, Christianity, Native American religions, or other faiths.

Rights and Responsibilities

You have read that governments provide services and enforce laws. State and local governments in New Mexico also perform other important jobs. One such job is organizing elections. In these elections, citizens of New Mexico who are 18 years old or older can vote for their government representatives.

Voting is one right that New Mexicans enjoy as citizens of our country and our state. A **right** is something to which you have a claim, or something you deserve. However, in the past some people in the United States did not have the right to vote. At times African Americans, Native Americans, women, and many Hispanic Americans have all been denied the right to vote. The passage of laws by Congress and the approval of amendments, or changes, to the United States Constitution eventually extended voting rights to these groups.

Many other important rights of United States citizens are guaranteed by the Bill of Rights of the U.S. Constitution. Such rights include freedom of expression, freedom of religion, and freedom of assembly. An assembly is a meeting or gathering of people for some purpose.

Freedom of expression is the right to say or write things without fear of being punished. However, this right does have limits. For example, you cannot say or write something about another person that you know to be false. Earlier in this lesson you learned that rules and laws help keep people safe. Limits placed on people's rights often serve the same purpose—to protect people.

Freedom of assembly means that people have the right to gather in groups to hold meetings and share their views. This is an important right. In some countries, people can be arrested for holding meetings or gathering to protest. To enjoy this right, groups must be peaceful. They also cannot perform any unlawful acts.

All of the rights guaranteed in the U.S. Constitution's Bill of Rights are also found in the bill of rights in New Mexico's state constitution. In fact, New Mexico's Bill of Rights lists additional rights that do not appear in the U.S. Constitution.

In addition to rights, New Mexicans also have important responsibilities. A **responsibility** is something that you have a duty to do. You have read that adult citizens have the right to vote in elections. However, citizens also have the responsibility to exercise this right. Citizens have other responsibilities too. These include serving on juries, paying taxes, obeying laws, and respecting the rights of others.

You have important responsibilities at your age too. These responsibilities include staying informed about important issues in your state and getting a good education. Acting responsibly today will prepare you for the future, when you will take on additional responsibilities.

REVIEW Identify one right and one responsibility of New Mexicans.
Main Idea and Details

▶ This is one of many places in Albuquerque where people go to vote. People stand at special tables set up along the sides of the room. They mark their votes on a ballot, or a piece of paper used in voting.

Good Citizenship

By practicing good citizenship, you contribute to the well-being of your community and our state. **Citizenship** is the rights and responsibilities of being a citizen. You contribute to the well-being of your community when you think not only of yourself but also of others around you.

People contribute in many ways. They may give their time, skills, or money to a community in order to make it a better place. Even as a young person, you have many opportunities to practice good citizenship.

For instance, you can volunteer at your school by tutoring a younger student. Your school may also sponsor a school or town project in which you could take part. In **Cochiti Lake,** students worked on a community project with adults. Together they dug out an area to be used as a community playground. They earned an award for their volunteer work.

As you have read, getting an education is an important responsibility that you can fulfill. In fact, this duty is so important that New Mexico law requires you to attend school until you are 18 years old. Getting an education is also important because it helps you become an informed citizen. Almost everything you learn in school will help you better understand the world around you. Education helps you contribute to your community, state, and nation. Education also helps you learn how to make a living when you get older.

To do things responsibly, you need information to help you make the right decisions. Reading books, newspapers, and magazines is a good way to learn about your community, your state, your country, and the world. You can also talk to family members, teachers, and friends about these things. It is important to be polite to other people and listen respectfully, even if you disagree.

▶ **Students practice good citizenship by volunteering for community projects. This clean-up project contributes to the well-being of their community.**

You can also practice good citizenship outside your school. For example, in Las Cruces student volunteers remove graffiti from the city on one Saturday of every month.

People in the Chupadero and Rio Medio Valleys near Santa Fe have worked together to clean up trash and collect fallen branches and leaves. These actions reduce the risk of fire in their communities. These are just some of the many ways in which New Mexicans act as good citizens in their communities.

REVIEW How can young people practice good citizenship in New Mexico?
🔁 **Summarize**

▶ Some young people volunteer to help fellow citizens in hospitals, senior centers, and nursing homes.

Summarize the Lesson

- State and local governments provide many important services to New Mexicans.

- Governments make laws and rules to keep order and to protect the people they govern.

- People have both rights and responsibilities. Acting responsibly is a mark of good citizenship.

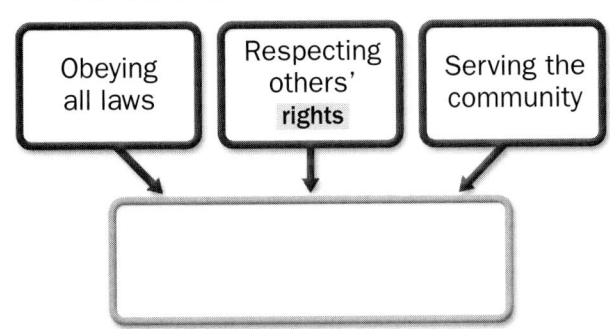

LESSON 1 REVIEW

Check Facts and Main Ideas

1. 🔁 **Summarize** On a separate sheet of paper, write a summary of the details shown below.

```
┌──────────┐  ┌──────────┐  ┌──────────┐
│ Obeying  │  │Respecting│  │ Serving  │
│ all laws │  │ others'  │  │   the    │
│          │  │  rights  │  │community │
└────┬─────┘  └────┬─────┘  └────┬─────┘
     │             │             │
     ▼             ▼             ▼
┌─────────────────────────────────────┐
│                                     │
│                                     │
└─────────────────────────────────────┘
```

2. How does the state of New Mexico serve its **residents?**

3. How would life in your community or in New Mexico be different if there were no rules or laws?

4. What is the difference between a **right** and a **responsibility?**

5. Critical Thinking: *Generalize* How can school and community projects encourage good **citizenship?**

Link to ⚭ Writing

Write a Speech Think of an important problem in your school or community. Write a speech to convince others to take action to help solve this problem.

Research and Writing Skills

Read a Newspaper

What? Newspapers are sources of information about what is happening now. They are usually printed daily or weekly. They can tell about events that have happened or that are coming up in your school, community, state, and country, as well as around the world.

Newspapers contain different types of articles. **News articles** give you facts about recent events. **Feature articles** give information about a person, place, or event of special interest to readers. **Editorials** give opinions about a subject, often one that is currently being discussed or debated.

Newspapers are organized into sections by type of article and subject. The **table of contents,** often on the front page, tells you where to find articles on different topics. The newspaper **headline** above each article gives you an idea of what the article is about. The **byline,** which is below the headline, tells you who wrote the article.

▶ **Want to know what is happening now? Read a newspaper and find out.**

Why? Reading newspapers is a good way to be informed about what is happening in the United States and around the world. You can research articles in old newspapers in the library to tell you about events in the past. Information you read in a newspaper might make you want to get involved with an issue or attend an event. Newspapers are also a good source of information about events that will happen in the future.

New County Park Opens
By Cathy Steinberg

Miller Field opened in Los Arboles on July 9. Mayor Laura DeLallo cut the ribbon during the opening ceremony.

More than 300 local residents came to the opening ceremony, which took place from noon to 2:00 P.M. In her speech, the mayor invited all people living in the county to enjoy the park. "The county's population has been growing rapidly," she said, "and we have needed more parks for people of all ages."

The county's citizens voted last summer to build the new park. Construction began in April of this year. Money to build the park came from taxes and donations from local businesses.

The park has a pool, basketball courts, and a baseball field. A playground with swings and slides is available for children. An indoor ice rink is located on the south end of the park for hockey and figure skating.

How? Read the article on this page. A well-written news article should answer these questions:

Who or *What* is the article about?
When did the event take place?
Where did it take place?
Why did the event happen?
How did the event take place?

Ask yourself these questions as you read the article again. Write your answers.

Think and Apply

1 Who wrote this article, and what is the line with the writer's name called?

2 Why is the opening of the new park such an exciting event for Los Arboles?

3 How can reading a newspaper help you find out past, present, and future information?

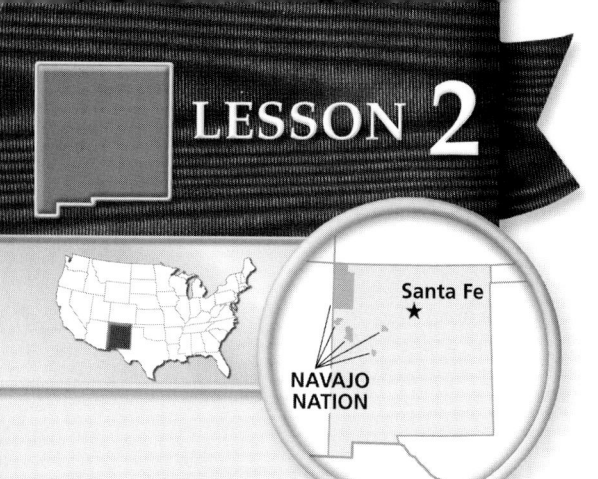
PREVIEW

Focus on the Main Idea
New Mexico has state, local, and tribal governments that provide services for people.

PLACES
Santa Fe
Navajo Nation

VOCABULARY
bond
interest
majority
bill
district
minority

TERMS
majority rule
public good

▶ The official opening of a new building often includes a ribbon-cutting ceremony.

Government for the People

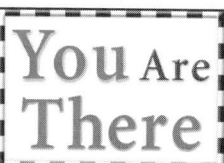

You Are There For several months you have watched workers building your city's new community center. As you walked to and from school, you saw it slowly rise from the ground. Now you and your school chorus are here to help celebrate the center's official opening.

The ceremony is starting. The mayor uses a pair of scissors to cut the red ribbon stretched across the center's main entrance. Someone raises the state flag on the flagpole nearby. You and the other members of your school chorus begin singing the state song. Soon you will hear the crowd cheer. Then everyone will tour the center for the first time!

Summarize As you read, look for details that help summarize how governments raise money to provide services for people.

How Governments Raise Money

Governments provide various goods and services. However, governments must raise money to pay for these goods and services. Two ways that governments can raise money is by taxing and borrowing.

Governments collect various kinds of taxes to raise money. When your parents buy groceries, a tax is added to the bill. In addition, people and businesses pay taxes on the amount of money they earn.

Local governments such as those in towns and cities also collect taxes. Most of their money comes from property taxes, or taxes on the value of land or buildings. Taxes on businesses also provide money for local governments.

Governments also can raise money by borrowing. Governments can borrow money by selling bonds. A **bond** is a kind of loan. The borrower promises to pay back the lender over time the amount lent plus interest. **Interest** is money paid for the use of someone else's money. Governments sell bonds when they need money for large projects. The buyers are repaid over several years. For repayments the government uses money collected from taxes or fees from the projects.

REVIEW What kinds of taxes do governments collect to raise money?
Main Idea and Details

▶ Bonds sold by local governments provide money to build new schools, such as this one in Albuquerque. They are also used to expand existing schools.

▶ New Mexico's capitol is nicknamed the Roundhouse because of its circular shape. It was patterned after the Zia sun symbol and represents a Pueblo kiva, or ceremonial center.

State Government

You learned in Chapter 2 that the capital of our state government is located in Santa Fe. It is the oldest capital city in the United States. The photograph above shows the state capitol building in Santa Fe.

Like our national government, our state government is divided into three branches. These branches are the executive, the legislative, and the judicial.

As you read about each branch, refer to the diagram on page 109.

The executive branch carries out and enforces laws. The governor heads the executive branch. The people of New Mexico elect the governor to a four-year term. By law, the governor of New Mexico cannot serve more than two terms. In addition to the governor, voters also elect other members of the executive branch. These elected officials help the governor manage New Mexico's state government.

FACT FILE

Symbols of State Government

Like other states, New Mexico has a state flag and a state seal. Both are based on New Mexico's history and rich traditions.

▶ New Mexico's state flag was adopted in 1925. It displays the colors of Spain and the ancient sun symbol of the Zia Pueblo. The circle on the flag stands for the sun. The rays represent the four compass directions, the four seasons, the four times of day (sunrise, noon, evening, and night) and the stages of life (childhood, youth, middle age, and old age).

▶ The state seal shows an American eagle protecting a smaller Mexican eagle. It represents New Mexico becoming part of the United States. The state motto, *Crescit Eundo,* means "It grows as it goes" in Latin.

Elections are based on majority rule. A **majority** means the larger number, or more than half. **Majority rule** means decisions are made according to what most people want.

The legislative branch makes our state's laws. New Mexico's legislature is made up of a Senate and a House of Representatives. Senators serve four-year terms. Representatives serve two-year terms.

A majority of members in each house of the legislature must vote to pass a **bill,** or proposed law. If the governor signs the bill, it becomes law. Sometimes the governor does not sign it. Then the legislature still can make the bill a law if two-thirds of its members agree.

The judicial branch of New Mexico's government explains the meaning of state laws. It decides whether laws have been broken. This branch is made up of different kinds of courts. Cases involving serious crimes may be heard in district courts. A **district** is part of a state or city marked off for a special purpose. District courts hear cases in which people disagree, such as arguments over property lines. A person who disagrees with a court's decision may take the case to a court of appeals. The highest court of appeals in New Mexico is our state Supreme Court. Its five justices are elected to eight-year terms.

REVIEW How is New Mexico's state government divided? ⟳ **Summarize**

New Mexico's Government

Legislative Branch

Makes laws
House of Representatives
Senate

Executive Branch

Carries out laws
Governor
Other elected officials

Judicial Branch

Interprets laws
Supreme Court
Court of appeals
District courts

▶ Each branch of New Mexico's government can be divided into smaller parts.

DIAGRAM SKILL *Which branch of the state government has courts?*

Local Governments

Three forms of local government exist in New Mexico. These include county governments, local city or town governments, and governments of special districts. You have read about districts for courts. School districts are another example of the many special districts in our state.

Of all the local governments, county governments serve the largest areas. Counties cover large areas of land and have many people to govern. Counties may include several cities, towns, and rural areas. The map on this page shows that New Mexico is organized into 33 counties. Many are quite large. Seven of the counties each cover more than 5,000 square miles of land. This is an area larger than the entire state of Connecticut.

Most county governments are run by a group called the board of commissioners. The commissioners are elected by voters. They perform duties such as deciding how much property tax to collect. They also decide how the county's money should be spent.

Some of New Mexico's courts are located in counties. County courts handle less serious cases than the state's district courts.

Another form of local government is found within the cities and towns of our state. Nearly all city or town governments have an elected mayor. A mayor manages the day-to-day operations of city or town government. This work might include appointing leaders, such as the chief of police. The mayor works closely with city

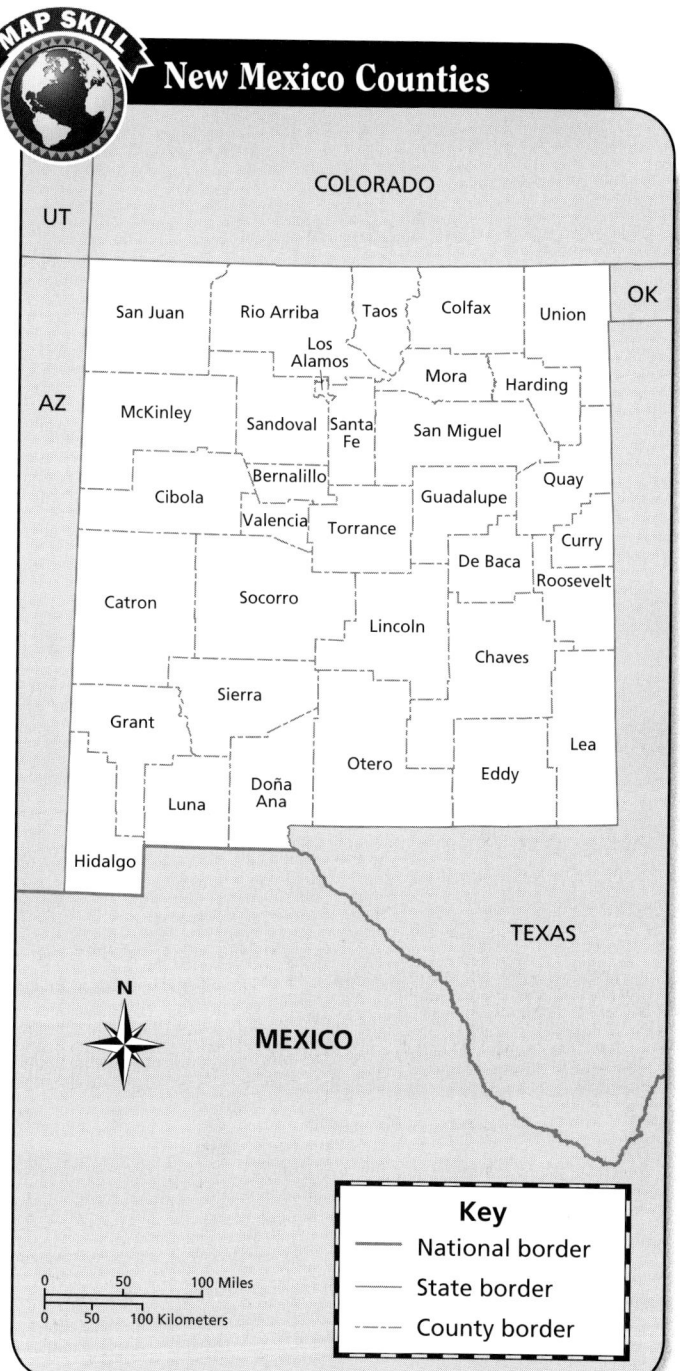

MAP SKILL New Mexico Counties

► Each county has a county seat, which is a town or city where county government is located.

MAP SKILL Location *Which counties are located along the northern border of New Mexico?*

or town councils to take care of the needs of the people in the community they serve. A council is a governing body that makes laws and spends tax money on various projects.

Special districts in New Mexico include public school districts. Each of our state's 89 public school districts is managed by a board of education. Voters elect its members. Each board hires a superintendent to manage the daily operations of the schools.

Our state also has soil and water conservation districts. In Chapter 1 you learned that New Mexico has a dry climate and limited water resources. As a result, soil and water conservation are very important. Voters elect people to a board that manages programs for carefully using soil and water.

In addition to state and local governments, there are many tribal governments in our state. You will learn about them next.

REVIEW What are the similarities and differences in the heads of county and city governments? **Compare and Contrast**

▶ The city council of Gallup meets regularly. In 2003 New Mexico Lieutenant Governor Diane Denish met with the council to discuss ways to develop small businesses.

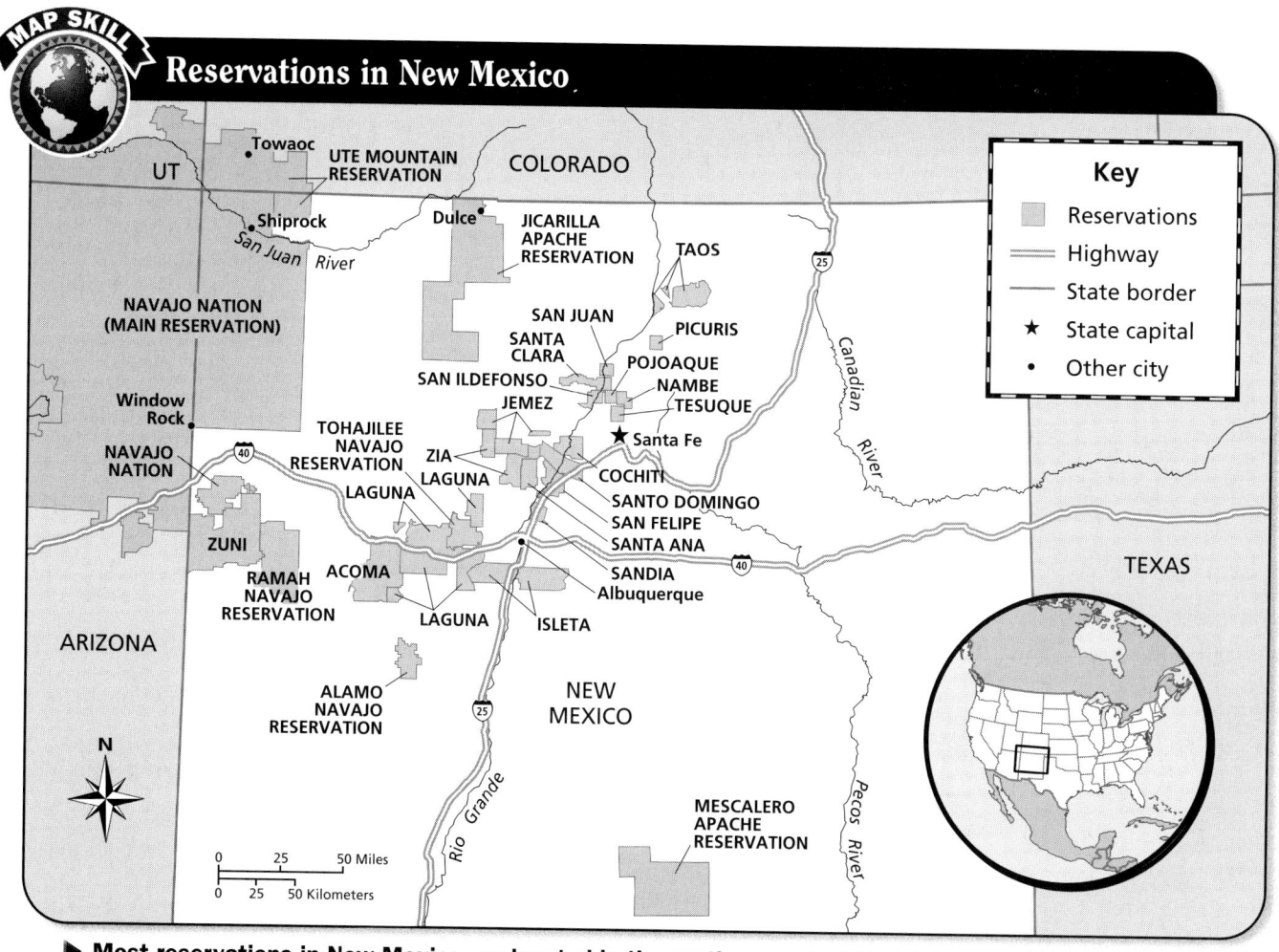

▶ Most reservations in New Mexico are located in the northern part of the state.

MAP SKILL Use Intermediate Directions *If you started at the Mescalero Apache Reservation, in which direction would you travel to reach the Zuni Reservation?*

Tribal Governments

As you have read, New Mexico has a diverse population. About one out of every ten New Mexicans is of Native American heritage. Some Native Americans live in urban or rural areas. However, many live on land that belongs to Native American groups. Reservations belonging to Pueblo peoples are located in our state. In addition, all or part of the reservations of the **Navajo Nation,** the Mescalero (mes kuh LAIR oh) Apache, the Jicarilla (hee cuh REE yuh) Apache, and the Ute Mountain are located here. In Chapter 2 you learned that reservations are land set aside by the U.S. government for Native Americans to live on.

Individual Native Americans living on tribal land are served by the tribal government. They also have the same rights as other United States citizens.

Native American tribal governments are separate from state and local governments. However, these governments have to follow certain rules established by the United States government. Each Native American government has the power to make laws, carry out laws, and decide whether laws have been broken. Tribal governments also have the power to set budgets, issue taxes, and control the use of tribal land.

There are different tribal governments among the Pueblo people. They are divided among different tribal groups to form pueblos or villages. Each of New Mexico's pueblos is a separate community with its own government. Some pueblos have written constitutions. Many elect their leaders. In a few pueblos, leaders are appointed in a traditional way. The elders in the community help choose the leaders. Elders are the older, respected members of the group.

New Mexico's pueblos belong to the All Indian Pueblo Council. This group runs programs for the pueblos in education, health, business development, and other areas.

Other Native Americans in New Mexico live on reservations. Each reservation forms one large community of people. The largest Native American reservation in the United States, both in land area and in population, is the Navajo Nation. Today Navajo people are usually called the Diné, but in 1969 they named their reservation the Navajo Nation. The reservation extends across three states—Arizona, Utah, and New Mexico. Other Navajo reservations in our state include the smaller Alamo, Tohajilee, and Ramah Reservations.

The Diné are governed by the Navajo Tribal Council. The Diné elect 88 council members. The council makes and enforces tribal laws. The Navajo Nation also has a president, a police force, and a court system.

The Mescalero and Jicarilla Apache also have tribal councils similar to that of the Navajo Nation. Council members are elected, and the council chooses the president and other leaders. The tribal councils of the Mescalero and Jicarilla Apache each have eight members.

A small part of the Ute Mountain Reservation extends from Colorado into northwestern New Mexico. The Ute Mountain Ute elect seven people to their tribal council. It has been their government since the Ute Mountain Ute wrote their constitution in 1940.

REVIEW In what different ways do Native Americans in our state govern themselves? **Main Idea and Details**

▶ Zuni pueblo government provides education at Zuni High School. Here students receive healthful snacks between classes.

▶ A tribal police officer patrols the Sandia pueblo to keep people safe.

PUEBLO OF SANDIA
POLICE

Governments Past and Present

The government of the United States is a republic. In a republic, the people elect representatives to make laws and run the government. Our national, state, and local governments work for the public good. **Public good** means the good of all the people, including minorities. A **minority** is a group within a country or state that differs in race or religion from the larger part of the population.

The land that is now New Mexico has had several different forms of government. Some forms involved self-government, such as Native American groups that govern themselves. At other times one group forced its power and its practices on others. The chart on this page describes some of the similarities and differences among these different governments.

You have learned that during the Spanish colonial period, New Mexico was ruled by a governor. The king of Spain or his representative in Mexico City appointed each governor. After Mexico gained its independence, the governor was appointed by the Mexican government. A council was formed to advise the governor, but it had no power.

New Mexico's Governments	
Government Type	**Features**
Spanish Colonial Government	*Apply the laws:* Governors carried out the law and served as judges *Majority rule:* No; the governor was chosen by the Spanish government *Public good:* Established roads
Mexican Colonial Government	*Apply the laws:* Town councils or appointed leaders served as judges *Majority rule:* No; the governor was chosen by the Mexican government *Public good:* Allowed trade with the United States
U.S. Territorial Government	*Apply the laws:* People have the right to trial by a jury of their peers, or equals *Majority rule:* No; governor and judges were not elected *Public good:* Encouraged industries such as railroads and mining to come to New Mexico
New Mexican State Government	*Apply the laws:* People have the right to trial by a jury of their peers, or equals *Majority rule:* Yes; state and local leaders are elected; voting rights are given to all citizens age 18 or older *Public good:* Built highway system and dams

▶ This chart shows some of the many changes in the government of New Mexico over time.

CHART SKILL *How did the various governments of New Mexico use majority rule?*

The U.S. government appointed territorial leaders after New Mexico became a territory of the United States. When New Mexico became a state, people elected their own leaders and representatives. Like its land and its people, New Mexico's government has had a long and colorful history.

REVIEW How did New Mexico's different governments apply laws?
Compare and Contrast

Summarize the Lesson

- Governments raise money to pay for goods and services by taxing and borrowing.

- The three branches of state and local governments pass laws, carry out laws, and interpret laws.

- Native American tribal governments are an important type of government in New Mexico.

▶ The Palace of the Governors in Santa Fe was the center of New Mexico's Spanish, Mexican, and U.S. Territorial governments. It was built in 1610. It is the oldest building used as a capitol in the United States.

LESSON 2   REVIEW

Check Facts and Main Ideas

1. ⟳ **Summarize** On a separate sheet of paper, write a summary statement that supports the details.

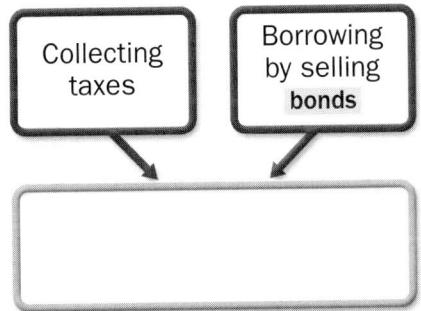

| Collecting taxes | Borrowing by selling **bonds** |

2. Explain the difference between the work of each branch of New Mexico's state government.

3. What local government bodies make laws, carry out laws, and decide whether laws have been broken?

4. What tribal government bodies make laws, carry out laws, and decide whether laws have been broken?

5. **Critical Thinking:** *Express Opinions* Which of New Mexico's governments do you think has provided the best benefits for the **public good?**

Link to   **Art**

Make a Campaign Poster Work with a partner. Suppose that your partner is running for school government. Make a campaign poster for him or her. Use slogans, or catchy phrases, and pictures to persuade others to vote for your partner.

Fort Sumner
Las Cruces

PREVIEW

Focus on the Main Idea
Many kinds of jobs and resources contribute to New Mexico's economy.

PLACES
Las Cruces
Fort Sumner

VOCABULARY
deposit

TERMS
checking account
savings account
high-tech industry
land use

▶ Money can be spent, saved, or borrowed.

New Mexico's Economy

You Are There
Today is an important day. As you enter the bank with your parents, you notice the many activities occurring there. A young couple is talking about buying a car. An older man wants to build onto his home. Like them, you have business at the bank. Today you are going to open a savings account. You have been saving the money you earn by doing small jobs for your family and neighbors. Now you have decided to put that money in the bank, where the amount of money can increase with interest.

Over time, you plan to add to this money, but for now things are just getting started. This will be your first deposit to your college fund!

Main Idea and Details As you read, look for ways that banks serve people and businesses in New Mexico.

Money and the Economy

Banks in our country serve many purposes. One of a bank's main jobs is to handle money. One form of money is currency, or coins and paper money. People and businesses make deposits in banks in New Mexico and across the United States. A **deposit** is money put in a certain place, such as a bank, for safekeeping.

People deposit money in different kinds of accounts. One such account is a checking account. A **checking account** is a bank account from which checks can be written to pay for products and services. People deposit money they plan to spend into their checking accounts. The money is kept safe, and people do not have to carry large amounts of cash.

When people spend money, it helps our economy. For example, when you buy a product, the store that sells it makes money. The store bought the product from a manufacturing company. That company makes money, and it pays the workers that produce the products.

People also help the economy by depositing money in savings accounts. A **savings account** pays interest. Banks use the money in savings accounts for loans. Businesses or people use the money loaned by the bank to buy something they might not otherwise be able to afford. In this way, banks act as go-betweens with savers and borrowers.

The people or businesses to which the bank loans your savings pay interest to the bank. The interest the bank charges them is higher than what it pays you. That is how a bank makes money through loans.

REVIEW What roles do banks serve?
Main Idea and Details

▶ Banks handle money for people through checking accounts, savings accounts, and loans.

117

Jobs and Workers

In Chapter 2 you read about some leading industries in New Mexico. Some of the same industries that grew here in the 1800s and 1900s are still part of our economy today. For example, the farming, ranching, and mining industries remain in New Mexico. Many New Mexicans continue to earn a living doing such work. However, over time some industries have grown a great deal while others have gotten smaller.

For example, the number of New Mexicans who work in mining has declined, or gotten smaller, since 1970. In recent years copper and potash mines in southern New Mexico have cut jobs. However, many workers who have lost jobs in shrinking industries have found new jobs in growing industries.

Today most New Mexicans work in industries that did not exist when New Mexico became a state in 1912. Job opportunities have continued to change throughout our state's history. The bar graph on this page shows how work in New Mexico changed from 1970 to 2000. The graph also shows that most workers in New Mexico today work in service jobs. People who work in service industries provide a service rather than produce crops or manufactured goods.

Many kinds of service jobs exist in New Mexico. Teachers and salesclerks are examples of service workers. Other examples include doctors, bus drivers, bank tellers, and auto mechanics. Travel is an important and growing service industry in New Mexico. It provides jobs throughout the state.

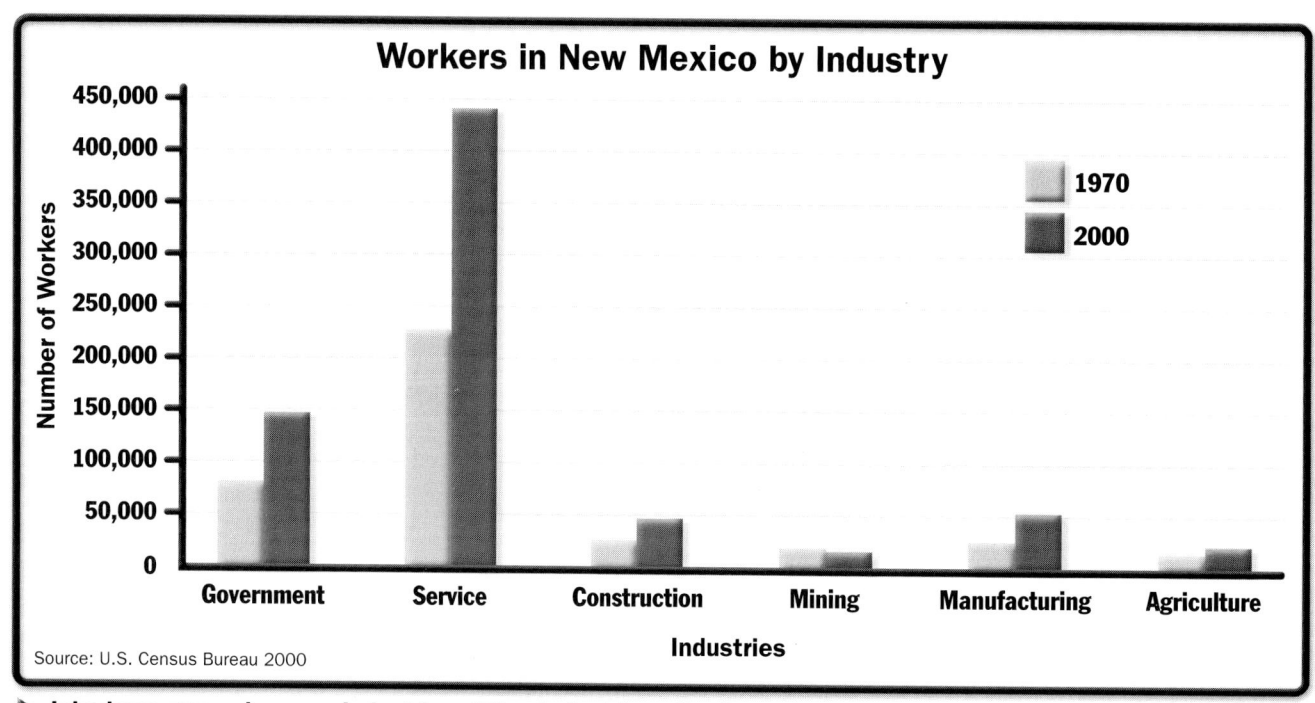

Source: U.S. Census Bureau 2000

▶ Jobs have grown in some industries. Other industries offer fewer jobs today.

GRAPH SKILL *What industry has the fewest workers in New Mexico today?*

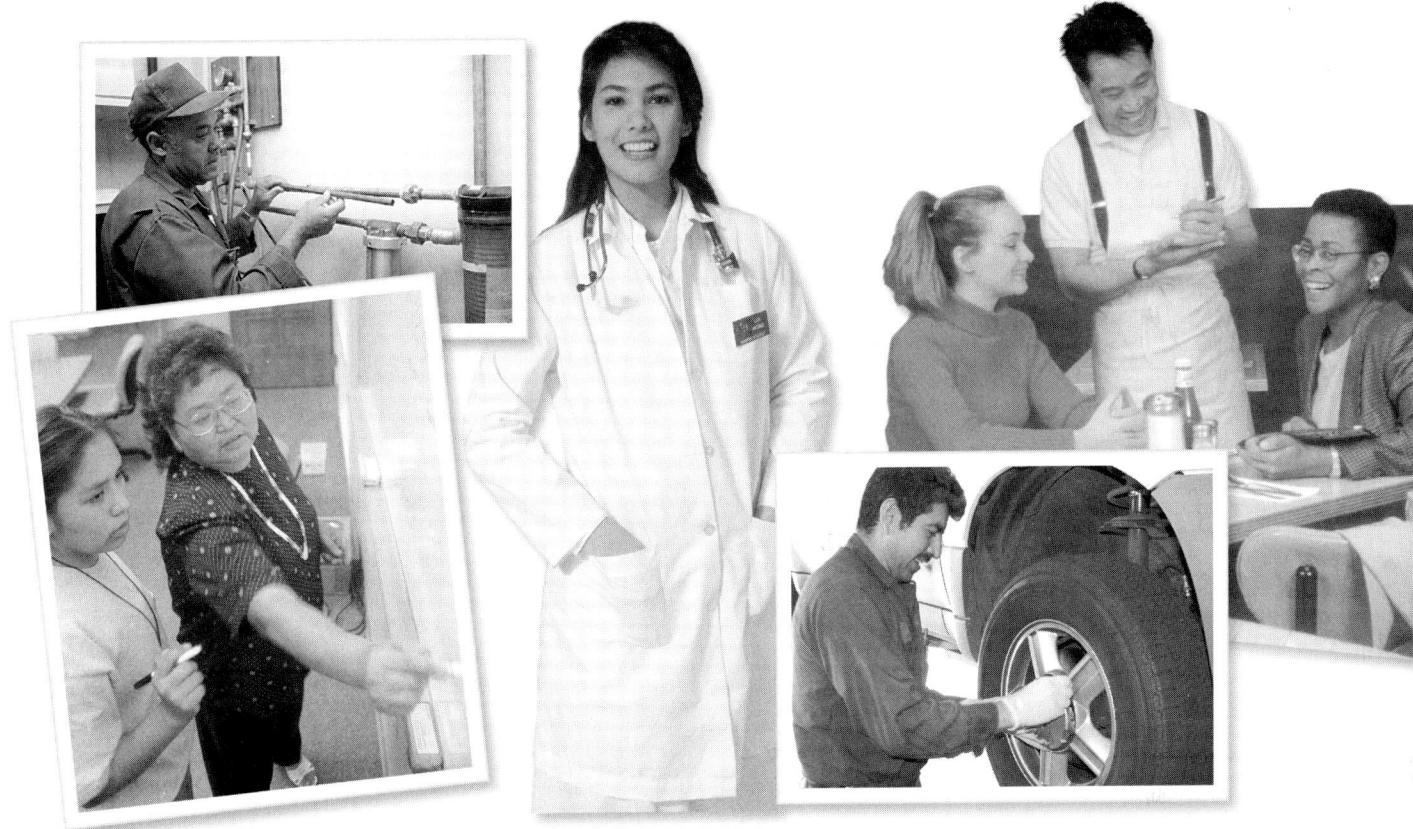

▶ These photographs show workers in various service industries such as education, plumbing, health care, food service, and auto repair.

Many of New Mexico's manufacturing jobs are in high-tech industries. A **high-tech industry** is one that uses the latest form of technology to make new goods and services. Telecommunications is a good example of a high-tech industry. It deals with sending messages by radio, telephone, and satellite. Telecommunications also is a very important industry in New Mexico. It provides thousands of service jobs.

In the early 1990s, the New Mexico state legislature lowered taxes on some businesses in the telecommunications industry. This helped bring new jobs to our state. In turn, companies began opening call centers in New Mexico to serve the telecommunications industry. Workers at these centers make or receive telephone calls from customers across the nation.

Other high-tech businesses have gained importance in our state. For instance, businesses that make computers and other electronic equipment employ about 30,000 workers in New Mexico. These industries are mainly in the Albuquerque area. Many high-tech companies also can be found in the area between Los Alamos and **Las Cruces.**

Government continues to be one of our state's largest employers today. About one in every four employees works for the government. Most government workers are employed at city or county government jobs.

REVIEW In what type of jobs do most New Mexicans work today?
Main Idea and Details

▶ A New Mexican farmer and his son walk by an irrigated field of lettuce.

Distribution of Resources

Water is one of New Mexico's most precious resources. But as you learned in Chapter 1, this resource is unevenly disributed throughout our state. Some places in New Mexico get little rainfall. Other places are located far from sources of water such as rivers. However, people's ability to get water does not change their need for it. Cities require large amounts of water. Farms, ranches, and industries do too.

According to state law, people in New Mexico do not own the water that is on, flows through, or lies under land. All water belongs to the state. People may use it, but how they use it is controlled by state law. For example, if you are the first person to take water from a source, such as a creek, you have the greatest right to it. But you can take no more than you need to use.

Later users of that creek have the right to take what is left under the same law. This process continues. Later users must buy a right to take some water from one of the earlier users.

REVIEW Describe how water is distributed throughout New Mexico.
⟳ **Summari**

Sharing and Using Resources

Sometimes resources must be shared. You have learned that water in New Mexico is limited and unevenly distributed. How is it decided who can use water and in what amounts?

Sometimes people work as a group to share water. They do this by forming an irrigation district. An irrigation district helps make sure that everyone gets water by dividing it among its members. Without irrigation districts, all available water might be gone before everyone in an area had received some of it.

An acequia association is similar to an irrigation district. Acequias have been used for many years. Although modern technology has reduced the need for these ditch systems, some acequias remain in use today in New Mexico. As with an irrigation district, an acequia association is run by an elected commission. The head of the commission decides how much water each family will receive. However, it is the community's responsibility to maintain the ditches.

Water is not the only limited resource in New Mexico. Deposits of coal, oil, and natural gas also are limited. These resources are burned to produce heat and electricity and will be used up someday. As a result, people in New Mexico are investigating other sources of energy. Wind is one such resource. Unlike the state's mineral deposits, wind is an unlimited resource, meaning that it cannot be used up.

One of the largest wind power sites in the world can be found in New Mexico. The New Mexico Wind Energy Center near **Fort Sumner** changes the strong winds of the eastern plains into a source of power. Blades on 136 huge windmills turn as the wind blows. A turbine, or kind of engine, creates electricity from this movement. These turbines can produce enough electricity to power up to 94,000 homes.

REVIEW Compare and contrast wind and other energy resources.
Compare and Contrast

▶ At the New Mexico Wind Energy Center, a crane lifts a huge propeller as a worker watches from the top of the windmill. The completed windmill will produce power from the movement of the wind.

Private and Public Projects

When resources are limited, people compete for them. Individuals and groups sometimes disagree about the best use for a resource. Some people may want a resource for a certain use. Others may want it for a different use. When competition exists for a resource as important as water, conflicts may develop.

For example, you have learned that Albuquerque's drinking water comes from an aquifer. Over time Albuquerque's need for water has grown with its population. As a result, the city wants to take some additional water from the Rio Grande. However, other places farther down the river also may need this water. In such cases state government must decide what is best for the public good.

Land is a limited resource too. Similar conflicts sometimes occur over **land use,** or what should be done with a piece of land. For example, much of New Mexico's land is protected as state or national forests and wilderness areas. Some people might want more freedom to cut down trees in such places. This might provide more lumber and more jobs in certain industries. Other people might want to preserve these areas for recreation.

Private Project and Public Project Advantages	
Private Project: Parking Garage	**Public Project: Public Park**
• Provides more places to park cars	• Provides a place to relax or play
• Reduces on-street parking	• Offers a place for recreation
• Provides jobs for parking attendants	• Provides jobs for park workers

▶ Land around the Los Alamos government building is a park that people can enjoy.

▶ This parking garage in Albuquerque is an example of the private use of land.

People may disagree over whether to use a resource for public or private projects. Building new homes makes it possible for a community to grow. But some people may want to preserve an area in its natural state so that wildlife will have a place to live.

When a business uses land to build a factory in a community, it creates new jobs. But what if that land were used to build a public park instead? Here the choice is between a private project, such as a factory, and a public project. New jobs benefit the community, but so does the park. Which land use is in the public good? Will the private project or the public project better serve the interests of the community?

Such questions are not easy to answer. However, people in New Mexico are working on these and other issues so that our state remains an attractive place in which to live and work.

REVIEW Why do conflicts sometimes arise over the use of resources in New Mexico? ◉ **Summarize**

Summarize the Lesson

- Banks handle money and serve as go-betweens with savers and borrowers.
- New Mexico's economy has changed from one based on mining and agriculture to one based on high-tech and service industries.
- Resources such as water may be unevenly distributed.
- New Mexicans have cooperated and competed to make the best use of limited resources.

LESSON 3 REVIEW

Check Facts and Main Ideas

1. Main Idea and Details On a separate sheet of paper, write details to support the following main idea.

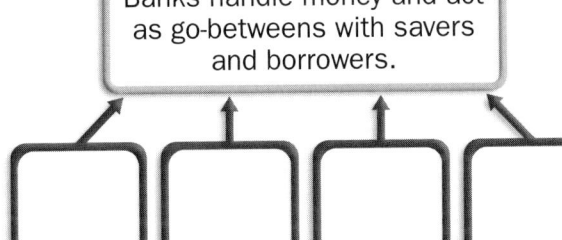

Banks handle money and act as go-betweens with savers and borrowers.

2. Identify industries from the 1800s and 1900s that have remained part of New Mexico's economy over time.

3. Explain why New Mexico's water resources are not equally distributed.

4. How are resources shared and used in new ways?

5. Critical Thinking: _Analyze Information_ How might a lumber company and a group of campers disagree on how to use forests?

Link to ⎯◦◦⎯ Economics

Research a Career Use your local library or Internet resources to find out about jobs in one of the industries discussed in the lesson, such as a **high-tech industry.** Prepare a report on your findings, and present it to the class.

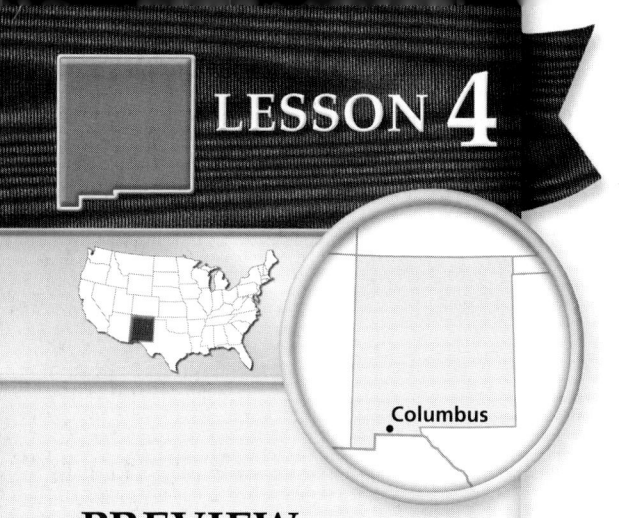

Columbus

PREVIEW

Focus on the Main Idea
People and products connect New Mexico to other states and countries.

PLACES
Columbus
Philippines

PEOPLE
Bill Richardson
Ralph Bunche

VOCABULARY
budget
market
tariff

TERMS
port of entry
NAFTA

▶ Our national legislature meets in the U.S. Capitol. New Mexicans there help make laws for our nation.

Links to Other Places

You Are There

The travel brochures are spread across the kitchen table. You are excited about your family's upcoming summer trip to our nation's capital, Washington, D.C. You are having fun making a list of the places to visit.

As you study a map of the United States, you notice the great distance between your home in New Mexico and Washington, D.C. You ask your mother how two places so far apart can be connected. "New Mexicans work in the national government," your mother says, "and they make sure that no one in Washington, D.C., forgets about New Mexico." You decide that the nation's capital doesn't seem so far from home. You can hardly wait to see the places on your list.

Main Idea and Details As you read, identify ways that New Mexico is connected to other places in our country and to other countries.

New Mexico and the Nation

In Lesson 2 you learned that our state government is set up like the government of the United States. New Mexicans elect leaders to represent them in the national government.

Three representatives and two senators represent New Mexico in the United States Congress in Washington, D.C. A representative is a person elected to act or speak for others. The map on this page shows New Mexico's three congressional districts. Voters in each district elect one representative to the United States House of Representatives. New Mexico's two United States senators are elected by our state's citizens.

Members of the United States Congress write our nation's laws and decide on the national government's budget. A **budget** is a plan for using money. New Mexico's members of the U.S. Congress work to help our state. They try to include money and jobs for New Mexico in the national budget. For example, military bases in New Mexico provide many jobs.

New Mexicans have held important positions in our national government's executive branch. For example, **Bill Richardson,** who was elected as New Mexico's governor in 2002, once

▶ One of New Mexico's military bases is White Sands Missile Range near Alamogordo. In 1982 the space shuttle *Columbia* landed there.

MAP SKILL — New Mexico's Congressional Districts

CO

San Juan · Rio Arriba · Taos · Colfax · Union · OK
Los Alamos · **3** · Mora · Harding
McKinley · Sandoval · Santa Fe · San Miguel
AZ · Bernalillo · Quay
Cibola · Valencia · **1** · Guadalupe · Curry
Torrance · De Baca · Roosevelt
Catron · Socorro · Lincoln
Chaves · TX
Sierra · **2**
Grant · Otero · Lea
Luna · Doña Ana · Eddy
Hidalgo · **N**

MEXICO

0 25 50 Miles
0 25 50 Kilometers

Key
─── Congressional district	─── State border
─── National border	--- County border

▶ New Mexico is divided into three congressional districts. Voters from each district choose one representative to send to Washington, D.C.

MAP SKILL Location *In which congressional district is San Juan County located?*

headed the U.S. Department of Energy. Before that, he represented the United States at the United Nations. The United Nations is an international organization to which many countries belong.

New Mexico has another connection to the United Nations. **Ralph Bunche,** who once lived in Albuquerque, had a long career with the United Nations. Bunche gained world fame when he was awarded the Nobel Peace Prize for his work.

REVIEW What elected leaders represent New Mexico in the United States Congress? **Main Idea and Details**

Linked by Trade

New Mexico's influence extends beyond its own borders and even the borders of the United States. One way its influence is felt is through trade. New Mexico's businesses trade with more than one hundred nations around the world. Trade includes exports, or items sent from one country to be sold in another. Trade also includes imports, or items brought from other countries to be offered for sale.

Other countries provide important markets for our state's exports, such as agricultural and manufactured products. In economics, a **market** is a country or area in which a company sells its goods. Goods move through **Columbus** and other cities located near our state's border with Mexico. Columbus is one of three New Mexican cities that are international ports of entry into New Mexico. **Ports of entry** are official places where travelers or goods enter or leave a country. Government officials carefully check goods and travelers moving through these ports of entry.

Mexico provides a key market for goods produced in our state. In addition, the United States has a trade agreement with both Mexico and Canada. It is called the North American Free Trade Agreement, or **NAFTA.** The agreement is designed to encourage trade between the United States and its two closest neighbors.

FACT FILE

Trade with Mexico and Canada

Imports from Mexico	Exports to Mexico
• Agricultural products and livestock	• Electrical equipment, computers, and electronic products
• Machinery and appliances	• Metal, plastic, and rubber manufactured goods
• Salt, sulfur, earth and stone, and plaster and cement	• Chemicals and fertilizers
• Furniture, cushions, and lamps	• Agricultural products and livestock

Imports from Canada	Exports to Canada
• Aircraft and aircraft parts	• Electrical equipment, computers, and electronic products
• Lumber	• Metal, plastic, and rubber manufactured goods
• Trucks and motor vehicle parts	• Transportation equipment
• Metal products	• Chemicals and fertilizers

Sources: New Mexico Economic Development Department; United States Department of Transportation; Canadian Embassy

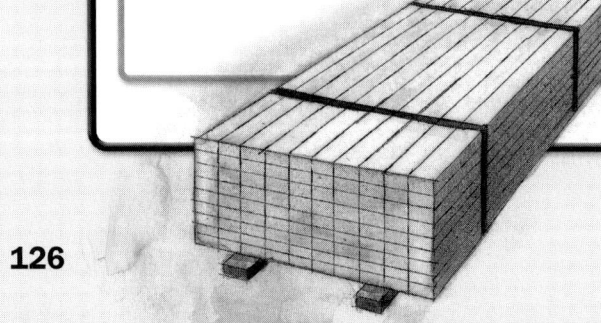

126

▶ The town of Columbus lies about 3 miles north of the Mexican border.

▶ At the Mexican border, police check vehicles as they cross into the United States.

One way that NAFTA encourages trade is by gradually reducing or removing tariffs among the three countries. A **tariff** is a kind of tax that is added to the price of imported goods.

The Fact File on page 126 lists some of the products that New Mexico trades with Canada and Mexico. You can see that New Mexico imports furniture from Mexico. Because of NAFTA, furniture can be imported into the United States very cheaply. That is because workers in other countries often earn less money than workers in the United States. As a result, employers in other countries can make and sell goods for less than companies in the United States. Some people believe that this is unfair. Some businesses have moved from the United States to other countries to take advantage of lower business costs. This has resulted in the loss of some jobs in the United States.

In addition to Canada and Mexico, New Mexico trades with many other countries.

However, it might surprise you to learn that New Mexico's top trade partner is the **Philippines.** This country in Asia lies off the southeast coast of China. This country buys more New Mexican products than Canada and Mexico combined. In fact, more than half of New Mexico's exports go to the Phillipines and other Asian nations.

Agricultural and mineral products from New Mexico also are sold to other countries. Besides livestock, our state's main agricultural exports include grains, tree nuts, and cotton. However, high-tech products and manufactured goods make up a much bigger part of the market. For example, in 2001 New Mexico exported about $20 million worth of minerals, oil, and natural gas. Exports of computer and electronic products that year amounted to more than $1 billion.

REVIEW What type of products does New Mexico export most?
Main Idea and Details

Resources Across Borders

In addition to trade, New Mexico and Mexico share water resources. A treaty between the United States and Mexico states that water from the Rio Grande must be shared by the two nations.

New Mexico also has water agreements with neighboring states. These agreements provide for a fair division of water among the states through which a river flows.

Without these agreements, there might be conflict over how much water different states use.

REVIEW Why do you think river water is divided among states and nations?
Draw Conclusions

Summarize the Lesson

- New Mexicans have elected representatives to the U.S. Congress who work to help the state.
- New Mexico has exported its products to more than 100 nations.
- A treaty and other agreements have required New Mexico and its neighbors to share water.

▶ Resources are not evenly distributed. The Rio Grande (left) brings water to New Mexico. The Niagara River (right) carries much more water as it flows between Canada and the state of New York.

LESSON 4 REVIEW

Check Facts and Main Ideas

1. **Main Idea and Details** On a separate sheet of paper, fill in the main idea that the details support.

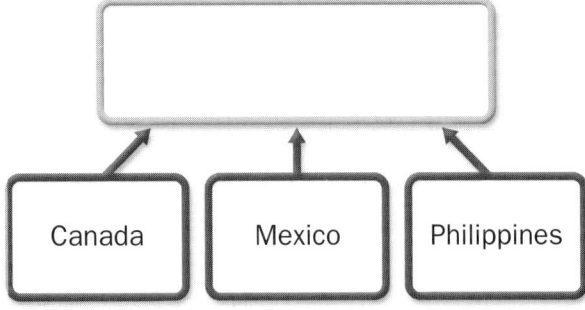

Canada   Mexico   Philippines

2. Compare how the state of New Mexico serves the interests of our country and of New Mexicans.

3. Explain how **markets** in New Mexico and in other parts of the world are linked.

4. Explain why resources may be unevenly distributed among states and nations.

5. **Critical Thinking:** *Analyze Information* What do you think might happen to the water in the Rio Grande if there were no treaty or state agreements requiring that it be shared?

Link to ⊶ **Art**

Make a Poster Research to identify an agricultural or manufacturing product in your area that is sold in another country. Make a poster with maps, drawings, and pictures that tells about the product and where it is sold.

Ralph Bunche
1904–1971

Ralph Bunche was born in Detroit, Michigan. When he was about eleven years old, his family moved to Albuquerque. His parents died about two years later. He and his two sisters moved to California with their grandmother.

Although Bunche only lived in Albuquerque for a short time, it was an important period in his life. His sixth-grade teacher's geography lessons sparked his interest in the world. In addition, Bunche was one of only two African American students in his class. During this time he got to know Hispanic and Native American students.

BIOFACT

In 1952 Bunche received the Horatio Alger Award. This award honors hard-working community leaders who help others.

Bunche went on to serve at the United Nations and to work for world peace. In 1949 he persuaded the leaders of Israel, Egypt, Jordan, Lebanon, and Syria to agree to end the war they had been fighting. He was awarded the Nobel Peace Prize for his efforts. He became the first African American to receive this great honor. Bunche believed that his experiences in Albuquerque shaped his belief in the rights of all people to peace, housing, education, and health.

"The real objective must always be the good life for all the people."

Learn from Biographies

How did Bunche's early experiences lead him to care about people?

Students can research the lives of significant people by clicking on *Meet the People* at **www.sfsocialstudies.com.**

■ Chama River Canyon

•Socorro

PREVIEW

Focus on the Main Idea
Many people contribute to New Mexico's culture and enjoy its beauty.

PLACES
Socorro
Chama River Canyon

PEOPLE
Leslie Marmon Silko

VOCABULARY
observatory

TERM
supercomputer

▶ A radio telescope

Science, Arts, and Recreation

You Are There

Dear Diary,
Today I finally visited the Very Large Array observatory. I had wanted to see it ever since we saw a story about it on television.

The antennas on this large radio telescope look like television satellite dishes, only much larger! Each dish-shaped antenna could easily hold two school buses. At the Visitor Center I learned that scientists use this telescope to learn about the universe. They can even use radio waves to make pictures of faraway stars and planets. It makes me proud to know that our state is making such important contributions to science and technology!

Main Idea and Details As you read, look for details about the scientific and cultural accomplishments of New Mexicans.

Science and Technology

The Very Large Array observatory is located west of **Socorro** on the Plains of San Agustin. An **observatory** is a building with equipment for watching and studying objects in space. The Very Large Array's 27 antennas form one of the largest radio telescopes in the world. A radio telescope is a large, dish-shaped antenna that can pick up radio waves from objects in space. Scientists use it to learn about some of the oldest stars in the universe.

The Very Large Array is one example of New Mexico's many contributions to scientific knowledge and technology. Scientist Robert Goddard is known as the founder of modern rocketry. He invented the first rocket motor that used liquid fuel. In the 1930s and 1940s he worked in Roswell, developing steering systems and many other improvements. Goddard's work allowed later scientists to develop missiles for defense and rockets to explore space.

One of those scientists was Clyde Tombaugh, who worked in the government's missile program at White Sands Missile Range. Later he started New Mexico State University's astronomy program. Astronomy is a science that deals with the sun, moon, planets, and stars. Tombaugh became famous for his discovery of the planet Pluto.

In 1972 New Mexico's Harrison Schmitt became one of the first scientists to work on the moon. He was an astronaut on the last United States mission to the moon in 1972. Schmitt later served New Mexico as a member of the U.S. Senate.

Today important research continues in New Mexico. For example, Sandia National Laboratory in Albuquerque is one of the nation's leaders in developing solar and wind energy. Similar research occurs in Los Alamos.

In Albuquerque, the University of New Mexico is one of the nation's leaders in developing supercomputers. A **supercomputer** is a very powerful, high-speed computer. The Lovelace Respiratory Research Institute is also located in Albuquerque. It is one of the largest independent medical research organizations in the United States.

REVIEW What sources of energy are New Mexican scientists helping develop?
Main Idea and Details

▶ The Very Large Array observatory has been operating since 1980. Each dish-shaped antenna measures 82 feet across. That is about as long as a basketball court.

Arts in New Mexico

Over time, people in New Mexico also have made important contributions to the arts. In fact, since the early 1900s many talented writers, painters, and other artists have lived in New Mexico. You read about some of them in Chapter 2.

Our state's legislature established the Department of Cultural Affairs in 1978 to promote, preserve, and celebrate the arts in New Mexico. These include visual, performing, and literary arts.

FACT FILE

Artists of New Mexico

Many talented artists have come from New Mexico or made the state their home.

▶ Peter Hurd grew up in Roswell but moved to the eastern United States to become a painter. He returned to New Mexico in the 1930s. Hurd was so impressed with the state's beauty that he spent the rest of his life here. He is known for painting the official portrait of President Lyndon Johnson.

▶ Navajo artist R.C. Gorman owns an art gallery in Taos. He is one of the nation's best-known Native American artists. Many art collectors praise his drawings and paintings of Native American women.

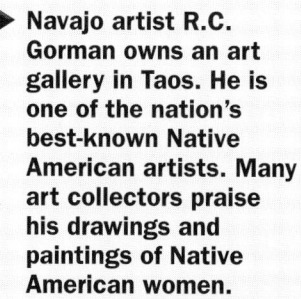

▶ Taos woodcarver Patrociño Barela was a santero, or an artist who creates sacred images. His famous carvings express New Mexico's rich Hispanic heritage. Barela's work has inspired many other artists.

▶ Pablita Velarde often paints pictures of traditional Pueblo life. She also writes and illustrates books. In *Old Father Story Teller*, Velarde retells Native American legends.

New Mexico is home to many famous writers, past and present. One of the best known is Tony Hillerman who lives in Albuquerque. Many of his detective novels feature Navajo police officers as their main characters.

Storyteller

by Leslie Marmon Silko

In this book of stories about her family, Leslie Marmon Silko includes a lullaby that her mother and grandmother sang.

The earth is your mother,
 she holds you.
The sky is your father,
 he protects you.
Sleep,
sleep.
Rainbow is your sister,
 she loves you.
The winds are your brothers,
 they sing to you.
Sleep,
sleep.
We are together always
We are together
 always
There never was
 a time
when this
was not so.

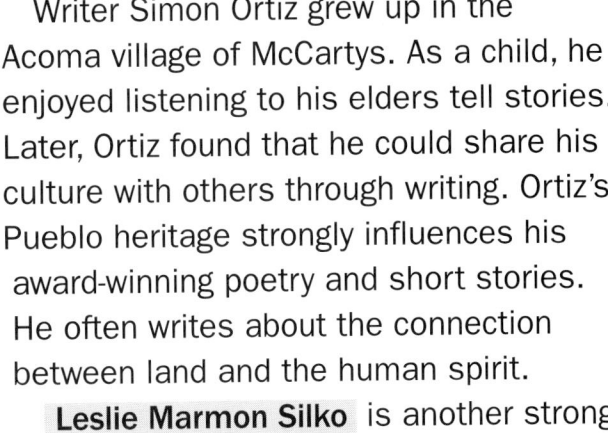

▶ **Leslie Marmon Silko**

Writer Simon Ortiz grew up in the Acoma village of McCartys. As a child, he enjoyed listening to his elders tell stories. Later, Ortiz found that he could share his culture with others through writing. Ortiz's Pueblo heritage strongly influences his award-winning poetry and short stories. He often writes about the connection between land and the human spirit.

Leslie Marmon Silko is another strong voice for Native Americans. She grew up on the Laguna Pueblo Reservation. There, with the help of her great-grandmother, Silko began a lifelong love of stories. In her novels and poems, she writes about Native American culture, history, myths, and traditions.

Ann Nolan Clark was born in Las Vegas in 1896. As a teacher, Clark found that Native American children needed books about their own culture. She then devoted much of her life to writing books to fill this need. In the 1940s, Clark lived and worked in many countries in Central and South America. She later used this experience to write books about children from these areas.

German guitarist and composer Ottmar Liebert moved to Santa Fe in 1986. The city's culture strongly influenced his music. He became famous by developing new musical styles. Other entertainers such as the late singer John Denver also have roots in New Mexico.

REVIEW What do New Mexican artists Tony Hillerman and Leslie Marmon Silko have in common? **Compare and Contrast**

Historic and Natural Places

New Mexico has many historic places to visit. Some include the remains of settlements of early peoples. Others preserve buildings from New Mexico's time as a Spanish colony and U.S. territory.

In Chapter 2 you learned about some historic places in New Mexico where early people lived. Chaco Culture National Historical Park is one of the largest ancient ruins in North America. Aztec Ruins National Monument, Bandelier National Monument, and Gila Cliff Dwellings National Monument are other ruins.

Historical sites from the Spanish colonial period include El Morro National Monument, Salinas Pueblo Missions National Monument, and Pecos National Historical Park. You read about El Morro in Chapter 1. The other two sites preserve what remains of some Spanish missions from the 1600s and 1700s.

If you are interested in New Mexico's history as a United States territory, you can visit the ghost towns of Kelly near Magdalena, or Winston or Chloride near Truth or Consequences. Fort Union National Monument and Fort Sumner State Monument both offer reminders of the days of United States conflicts with Native Americans.

The town of Lincoln is a National Historic Landmark. It gives visitors a view of what life was like in the 1800s. Lincoln was not always as peaceful as it seems today. Interesting characters from the Old West used to walk the streets. In 1881 the famous outlaw Billy the Kid escaped from the jail in the Lincoln County Courthouse.

People who enjoy beautiful mountains have many choices in New Mexico. The Jemez Mountains are close to both Albuquerque and Santa Fe. Their location offers hiking and camping opportunities for much of the state's population. To the north, visitors to the **Chama River Canyon** can enjoy canoeing, fishing, and hiking. This area is also a good place to see bears, elk, and mountain lions.

Wildlife such as bears, elk, and bighorn sheep also can be found in the Pecos Wilderness of the Sangre de Cristo Mountains. In the central Rio Grande region, the Sandia Mountains and the Manzano Mountains both offer wilderness areas for people in New Mexico to explore.

REVIEW What can visitors learn about New Mexico from its historic places?
Main Idea and Details

▶ **The Lincoln County Courthouse looks much the same today as it did in the 1800s.**

Map Adventure

New Mexico's Historical Sites

You have decided to travel around New Mexico in order to learn more about its history. You start from your home in Las Cruces.

1. The first site you want to visit is El Morro National Monument. In which direction will you travel?

2. You next decide to visit Fort Union National Monument. What river will you cross on the way?

3. From there you want to travel to northwestern New Mexico to visit three sites where early people lived. What are these three sites?

4. In which direction will you then travel to visit Gila Cliff Dwellings National Monument?

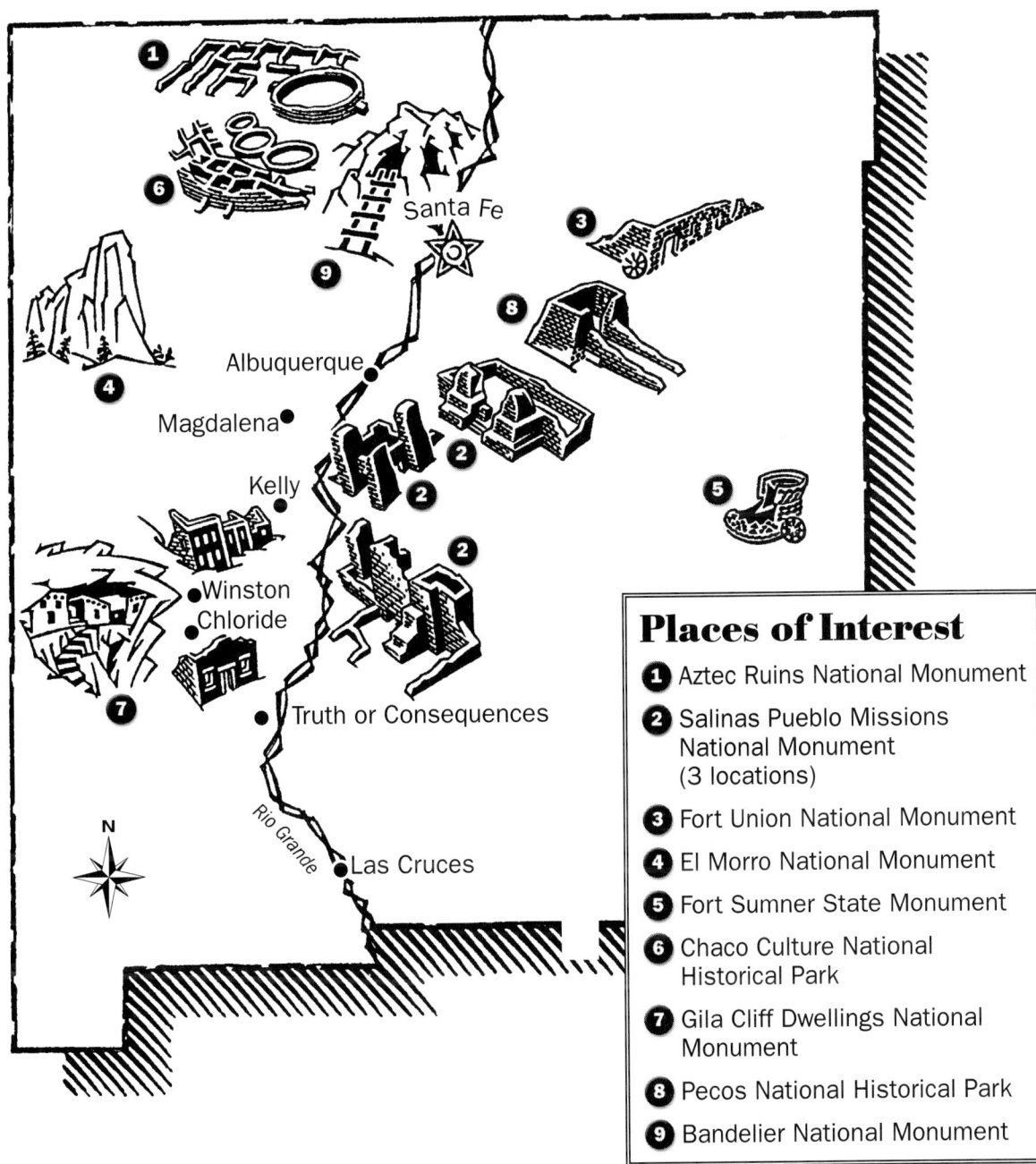

Santa Fe

Albuquerque

Magdalena

Kelly

Winston
Chloride

Truth or Consequences

Rio Grande

Las Cruces

N

Places of Interest

1 Aztec Ruins National Monument

2 Salinas Pueblo Missions National Monument (3 locations)

3 Fort Union National Monument

4 El Morro National Monument

5 Fort Sumner State Monument

6 Chaco Culture National Historical Park

7 Gila Cliff Dwellings National Monument

8 Pecos National Historical Park

9 Bandelier National Monument

At Play in New Mexico

New Mexico's many days of sunshine each year provide people throughout our state with opportunities to enjoy outdoor activities. Hiking and bike trails cross the state. Many of our state's rivers and lakes offer great fishing. The San Juan River attracts fishers from around the world. Whitewater boaters run the rapids of the Rio Grande Gorge. For people seeking more relaxed boating, the Rio Chama offers gentler rides.

Would you believe that snow skiing is popular in such a hot and dry state as New Mexico? It is true. Mountain ranges around the state offer world-class skiing.

New Mexico also has a rich athletic history. Golf is a popular sport here. Many cities have public golf courses on which residents can play. Nancy Lopez grew up playing golf on a public course in Roswell. At age twelve, she became New Mexico's

▶ Roy Cooper won the world championship in calf roping at the National Finals Rodeo in 1982.

▶ Nancy Lopez was named to the World Golf Hall of Fame in 1989.

women's amateur golf champion. Lopez went on to become one of the greatest professional women golfers of all time.

Rodeo is a popular sport with roots in ranching and cowhand skills. Today bronc riding, barrel racing, and calf roping are some of the events at the New Mexico State Fair Rodeo in Albuquerque. Roy Cooper of Hobbs is one of New Mexico's rodeo champions.

Many other athletes have achieved success in sports. Santa Rita's Ralph Kiner played major league baseball in the 1940s and 1950s. He entered the National Baseball Hall of Fame in 1975. In 1972 eighteen-year-old swimmer Cathy Carr of Albuquerque became the first New Mexican to win an Olympic gold medal. Racecar drivers Al Unser, Al Unser, Jr., and Bobby Unser also are from Albuquerque. They have won many auto races around the nation.

New Mexico is a land where people of many backgrounds have found success. Here different peoples have shared their cultures to form a single culture that is like no other. Here art and science continue to develop surrounded by great natural beauty. New Mexico is special. It truly is the Land of Enchantment.

REVIEW Summarize reasons why New Mexico is called the Land of Enchantment. ⟳ **Summarize**

Summarize the Lesson

• Major scientific research and developments have been achieved in New Mexico.

• Artists, writers, musicians, and athletes from New Mexico have gained recognition for their accomplishments.

• New Mexico's historic sites and natural places have reflected the state's long history and rich resources.

▶ Colorful sunsets add beauty to the Land of Enchantment.

LESSON 5 · REVIEW

Check Facts and Main Ideas

1. Main Idea and Details On a separate sheet of paper, fill in details that support the main idea.

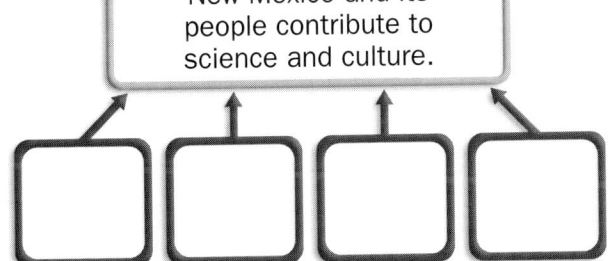

New Mexico and its people contribute to science and culture.

2. Name some New Mexican artists and writers who have gained recognition for their work.

3. Identify ways in which New Mexicans relate to the state's natural places in their free time.

4. Identify two people who represent New Mexico through sports.

5. Critical Thinking: *Apply Information* How do New Mexico's many historical sites illustrate the state's long and varied history?

Link to ⟷ **Writing**

Design a Pamphlet Choose one of the historic sites discussed in the lesson, and design a pamphlet that tells about it. Include a map to the site and drawings of some of its features along with your written description.

Chapter Summary

 Summarize
On a separate sheet of paper write details from this chapter that support the summary sentence.

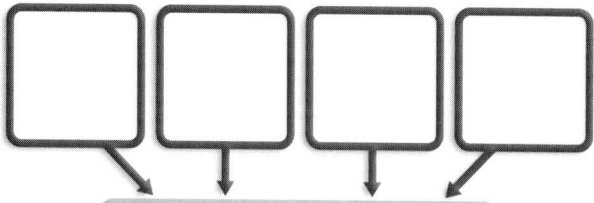

New Mexico's government, people, economy, and natural beauty make the state a great place to live.

Main Ideas and Skills

1 Why do governments collect taxes?

2 How are water rights decided in New Mexico?

3 **Main Idea** What does each branch of state government do?

4 **Main Idea** How does trade tie New Mexico to other countries?

5 **Critical Thinking: *Point of View*** What do you think New Mexico needs to do to make sure that it will remain a great place to live in the future?

Apply Skills

6 **Read a Newspaper** Reread the newspaper article on p. 105. How does the article answer some or all of the questions *Who? What? When? Where? Why?* and *How?*

Places and People

Match each place or person with the correct description.

1 **Santa Fe** (p. 108)

2 **Navajo Nation** (p. 112)

3 **Las Cruces** (p. 119)

4 **Bill Richardson** (p. 125)

5 **Ralph Bunche** (p. 125)

a. city with many high-tech companies

b. governor of New Mexico elected in 2002

c. Nobel Peace Prize winner

d. oldest capital city in the United States

e. largest Native American reservation in the United States

Use each of the following vocabulary words in a sentence that makes the word's meaning clear.

6 responsibility (p. 101)

7 interest (p. 107)

8 deposit (p. 117)

9 budget (p. 125)

10 market (p. 126)

Write About Government

1 **Write a letter** to the mayor or county commissioners. Identify a need in your community, and suggest in your letter how government should respond to it.

2 **Write an editorial** that encourages the state government to establish a New Mexico Achievement Day. In your editorial identify one New Mexican who you think should be honored, and explain why.

3 **Write an introduction** about citizenship for a school handbook. Describe the responsibilities of being a good citizen in your school.

End with a Song

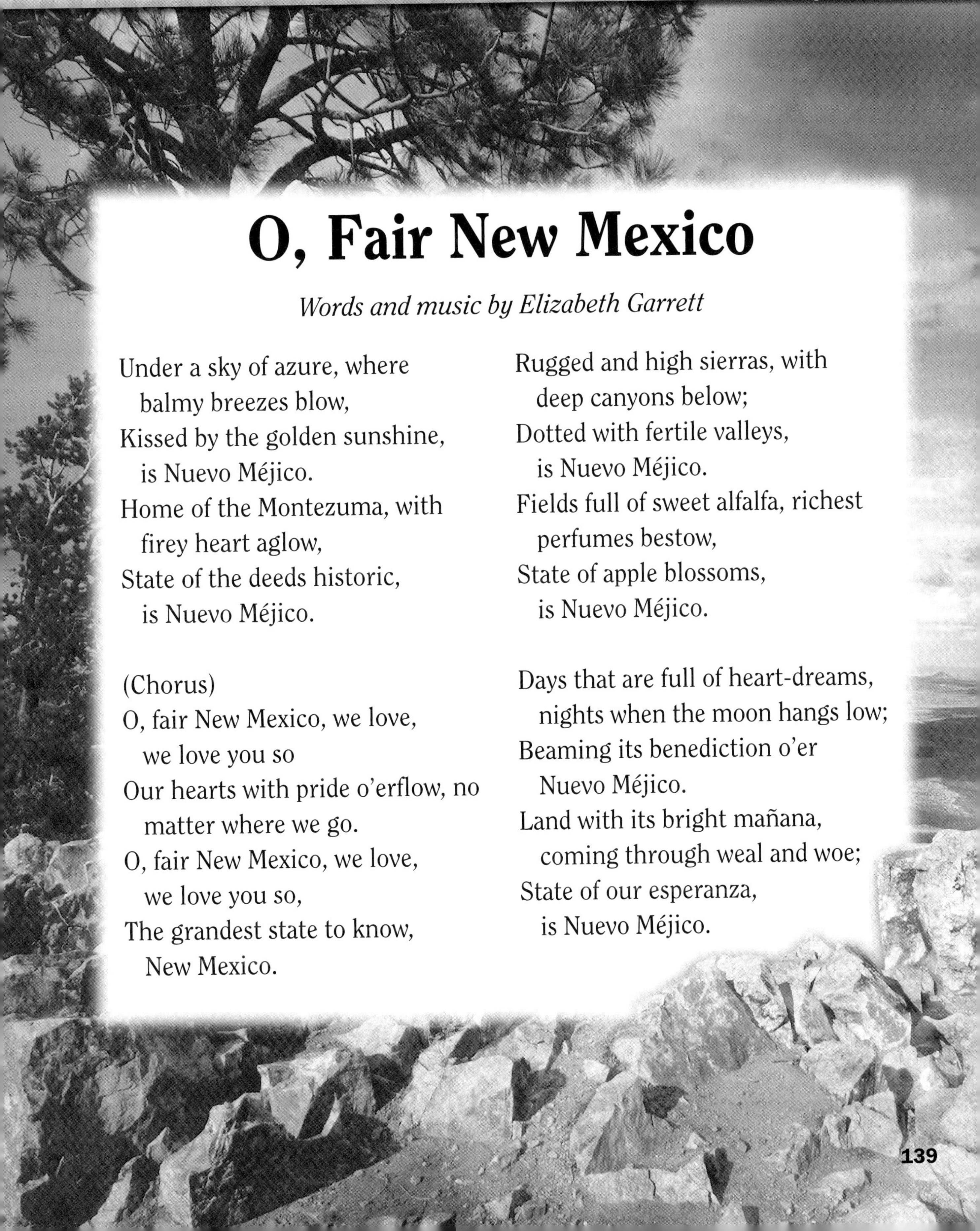

O, Fair New Mexico

Words and music by Elizabeth Garrett

Under a sky of azure, where
   balmy breezes blow,
Kissed by the golden sunshine,
   is Nuevo Méjico.
Home of the Montezuma, with
   firey heart aglow,
State of the deeds historic,
   is Nuevo Méjico.

(Chorus)
O, fair New Mexico, we love,
   we love you so
Our hearts with pride o'erflow, no
   matter where we go.
O, fair New Mexico, we love,
   we love you so,
The grandest state to know,
   New Mexico.

Rugged and high sierras, with
   deep canyons below;
Dotted with fertile valleys,
   is Nuevo Méjico.
Fields full of sweet alfalfa, richest
   perfumes bestow,
State of apple blossoms,
   is Nuevo Méjico.

Days that are full of heart-dreams,
   nights when the moon hangs low;
Beaming its benediction o'er
   Nuevo Méjico.
Land with its bright mañana,
   coming through weal and woe;
State of our esperanza,
   is Nuevo Méjico.

Unit Review

Main Ideas and Vocabulary

Read the passage below, and use it to answer the questions that follow.

New Mexico's geography and climate influence the people, plants, and animals that live here. Each plant and animal finds the kind of <u>environment</u> it needs to survive. People find beauty in the mountains, valleys, deserts, and grasslands. The land provides natural resources that people need to live. A sunny, warm, and dry climate also draws people to our state.

People throughout our state's history have depended on the land. Native American groups such as the Pueblo lived near rivers and farmed. The Diné and the Apache were hunter-gatherers who came to this area. Beginning in the 1500s, Spanish explorers and settlers established communities and farms along the Rio Grande. After New Mexico became a United States territory, prospectors and ranchers came to make a living. New Mexico continued to grow and became our nation's forty-seventh state in 1912.

Today New Mexico features diverse cultural traditions and varied job opportunities. Festivals throughout the state highlight the music, dances, foods, and crafts of Native American, Hispanic, and other cultures. The work of artists and writers helps increase awareness of New Mexico's heritage. Other workers find jobs in service industries such as tourism or in <u>high-tech industries</u> such as telecommunications. New Mexico's beauty, history, and unique culture make it a great place to live.

1 In this passage, <u>environment</u> means
   A water that flows or seeps downward, soaks the rock below the soil, and supplies springs and wells.
   B the land used by prospectors and ranchers to make a living.
   C all the surrounding things, conditions, and influences affecting the growth of living things.
   D anything made by human skill or work, especially a tool or weapon.

2 The main idea of the first paragraph is that New Mexico's
   A climate makes it difficult for plants and animals to survive.
   B geography and climate affect the lives of people, plants, and animals.
   C mountains and valleys are heavily populated.
   D diverse cultural traditions are featured in many different festivals.

3 You learn from the second paragraph that
   A Native Americans prospected for minerals.
   B the Rio Grande flooded many Spanish settlements.
   C the land has supported many different groups of people.
   D New Mexico's workers find jobs in service industries.

4 In this passage, the term <u>high-tech industries</u> means
   A industries that manufacture construction equipment.
   B industries that build factories at high elevations.
   C industries that produce costly products.
   D industries that use advanced modern technology.

People and Vocabulary

Match each word or person with the correct definition or description.

1 Georgia O'Keeffe (p. 11)

2 tributary (p. 13)

3 suburb (p. 43)

4 Popé (p. 60)

5 Zebulon Pike (p. 67)

6 bill (p. 109)

7 market (p. 126)

a. a type of community located near a large city

b. the Pueblo leader who organized the Pueblo Revolt against the Spanish in 1680

c. an artist who painted landscapes of New Mexico

d. a country or area where a company sells its goods

e. a proposed law

f. a stream or river that flows into a larger river

g. led a U.S. expedition, which entered New Mexico in 1807

Write and Share

Time Capsule Stories Write an essay about your life today in New Mexico. Suppose that people will read your essay fifty years from now. Include descriptive details so that the reader can learn what life in New Mexico was like at your time in history.

Read on Your Own

Look for these books in the library.

Apply Skills

Read a Newspaper to Learn About New Mexico
Find an article discussing an important event or issue in New Mexico today. Then design a poster that displays the information from the article. On your poster include the answers that the article gave to the questions *who, what, when, where, why,* and *how.* At the bottom of the poster, identify the headline, the author, and the type of article you selected.

Reference Guide

Table of Contents

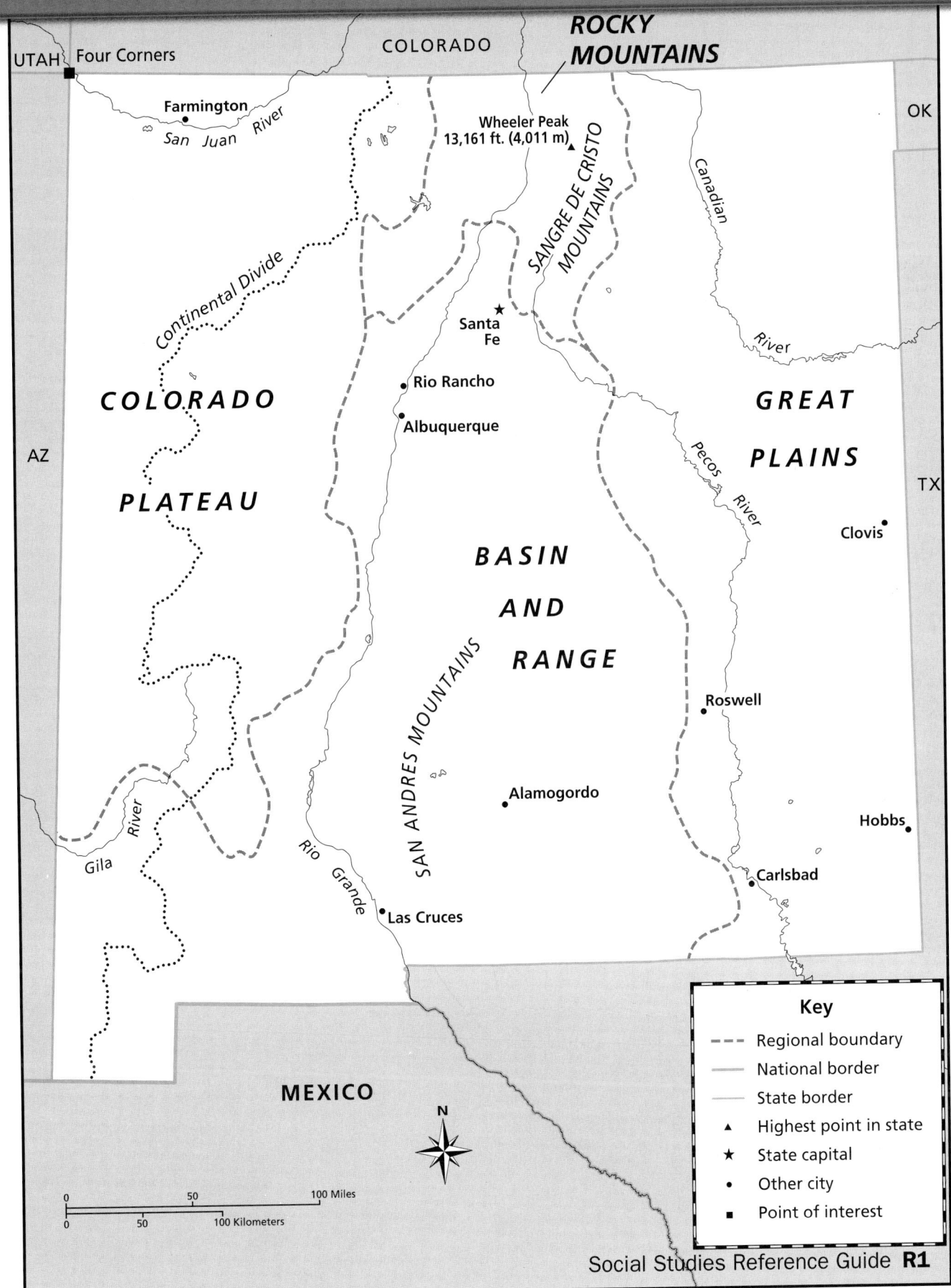

ROCKY MOUNTAINS

UTAH Four Corners
COLORADO
OK

Farmington
San Juan River

Wheeler Peak
13,161 ft. (4,011 m)

SANGRE DE CRISTO MOUNTAINS

Canadian River

AZ

Continental Divide

COLORADO

Santa Fe

Rio Rancho

Albuquerque

PLATEAU

GREAT

PLAINS

TX

Pecos River

BASIN

AND

RANGE

Clovis

SAN ANDRES MOUNTAINS

Roswell

Alamogordo

Hobbs

Gila River

Rio Grande

Carlsbad

Las Cruces

MEXICO

N

Key

- - - Regional boundary
—— National border
—— State border
▲ Highest point in state
★ State capital
● Other city
■ Point of interest

0   50   100 Miles
0   50   100 Kilometers

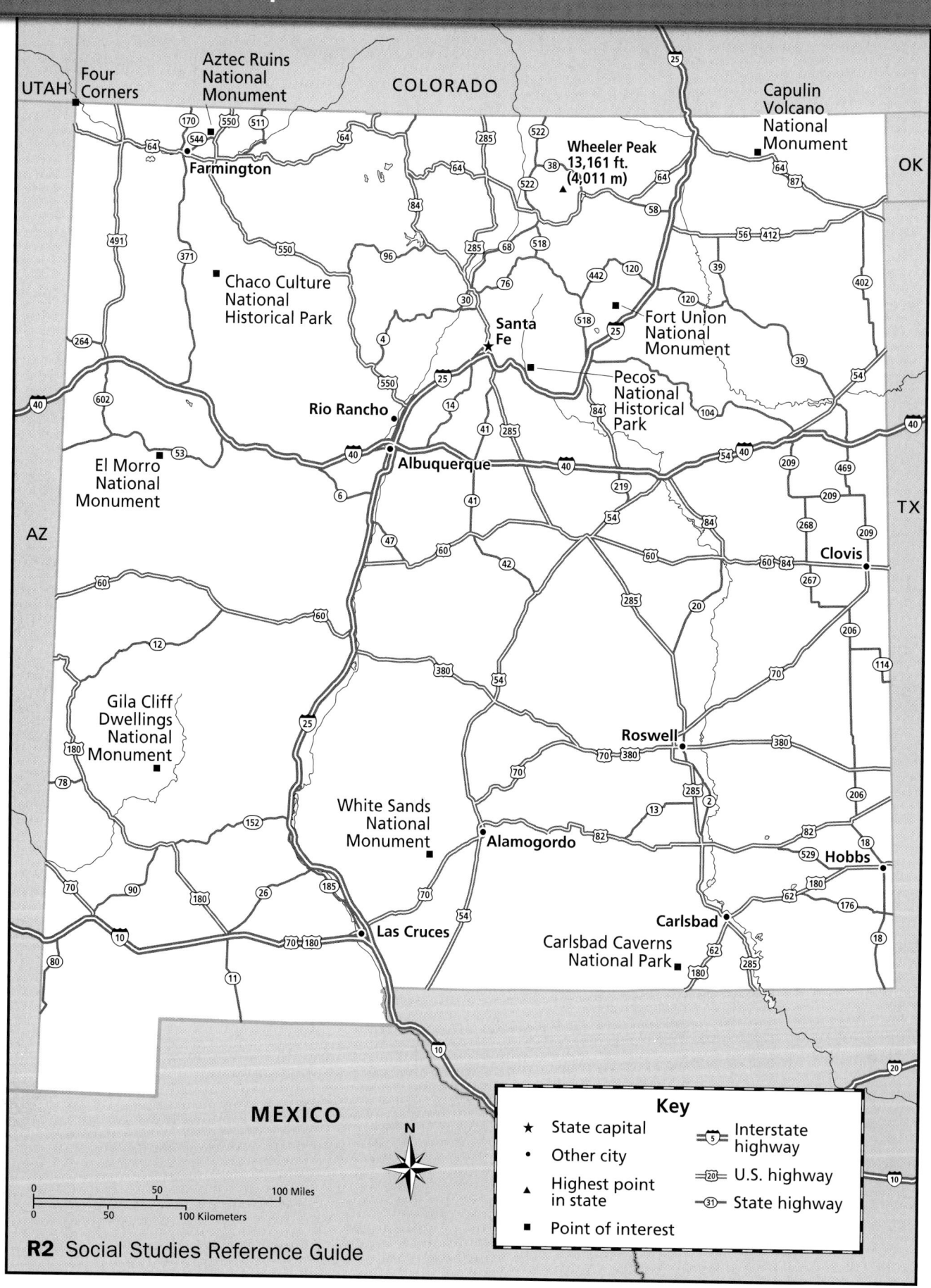

UTAH
Four Corners
Aztec Ruins National Monument
COLORADO
Capulin Volcano National Monument
OK

170   544   550   511
64
285
522
64
Wheeler Peak 13,161 ft. (4,011 m)
64
87
64
Farmington
38
522
58
56   412

491
371
550
96
285
68
518
442   120
39
120
402

264
4
30
76
518
Fort Union National Monument
39
54

Chaco Culture National Historical Park
Santa Fe
25
Pecos National Historical Park
84
104
40

602
550
14
25

40
Rio Rancho
41   285
219
84
209   469
TX

El Morro National Monument
53
40
Albuquerque
40
54   40
209

AZ
6
41
54
268
209

47
60
60
84
Clovis
60   84

42
267

60
285
20
206

12
380
54
114

Gila Cliff Dwellings National Monument
180
25
70
380
Roswell
380

78
70   380

152
White Sands National Monument
13
2
285
82
206

70
90
26
185
Alamogordo
82
529   Hobbs   18

80
180
70
54
62   180   176
62

11
Las Cruces
70   180
Carlsbad
18

MEXICO
Carlsbad Caverns National Park
62   285
180

10

N

Key

★ State capital
• Other city
▲ Highest point in state
■ Point of interest

5 Interstate highway
20 U.S. highway
31 State highway

0   50   100 Miles
0   50   100 Kilometers

Atlas
New Mexico Counties Map

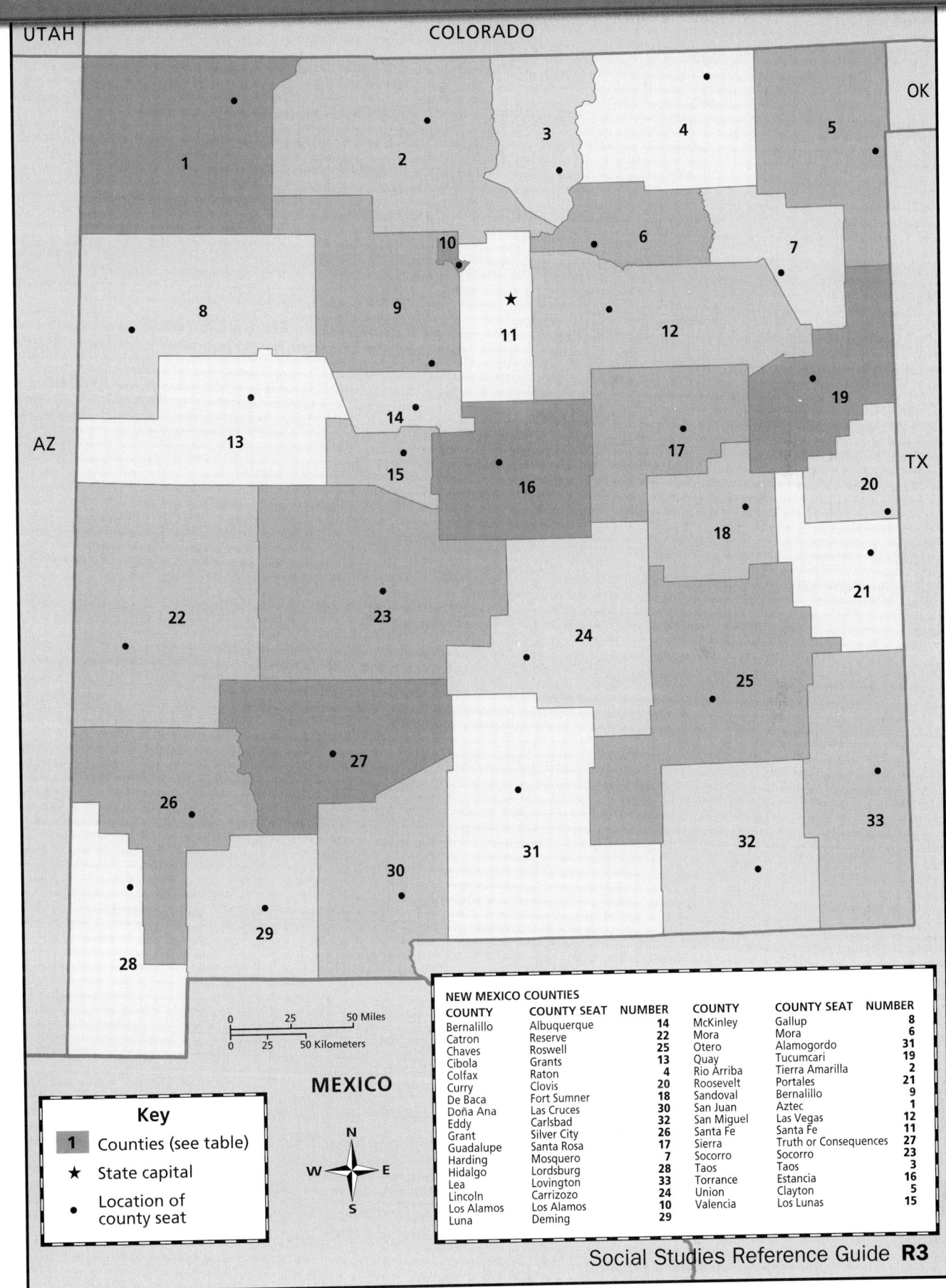

UTAH

COLORADO

OK

AZ

TX

MEXICO

1
2
3
4
5
6
7
8
9
10
11 ★
12
13
14
15
16
17
18
19
20
21
22
23
24
25
26
27
28
29
30
31
32
33

COUNTY	COUNTY SEAT	NUMBER
Bernalillo	Albuquerque	14
Catron	Reserve	22
Chaves	Roswell	25
Cibola	Grants	13
Colfax	Raton	4
Curry	Clovis	20
De Baca	Fort Sumner	18
Doña Ana	Las Cruces	30
Eddy	Carlsbad	32
Grant	Silver City	26
Guadalupe	Santa Rosa	17
Harding	Mosquero	7
Hidalgo	Lordsburg	28
Lea	Lovington	33
Lincoln	Carrizozo	24
Los Alamos	Los Alamos	10
Luna	Deming	29

NEW MEXICO COUNTIES

COUNTY	COUNTY SEAT	NUMBER
McKinley	Gallup	8
Mora	Mora	6
Otero	Alamogordo	31
Quay	Tucumcari	19
Rio Arriba	Tierra Amarilla	2
Roosevelt	Portales	21
Sandoval	Bernalillo	9
San Juan	Aztec	1
San Miguel	Las Vegas	12
Santa Fe	Santa Fe	11
Sierra	Truth or Consequences	27
Socorro	Socorro	23
Taos	Taos	3
Torrance	Estancia	16
Union	Clayton	5
Valencia	Los Lunas	15

0   25   50 Miles
0   25   50 Kilometers

Key

1   Counties (see table)

★   State capital

•   Location of county seat

N
W   E
S

Social Studies Reference Guide **R3**

New Mexico Governors

William McDonald
1912–1916

Ezequiel Cabeza de Baca
1917

Washington Lindsey
1917–1918

Octaviano Larrazolo
1919–1920

Merritt Mechem
1921–1922

James Hinkle
1923–1924

Arthur Hannett
1925–1926

Richard Dillon
1927–1930

Arthur Seligman
1931–1933

Andrew Hockenhull
1933–1934

Clyde Tingley
1935–1938

John Miles
1939–1942

John Dempsey
1943–1946

Thomas Mabry
1947–1950

Edwin Mechem
1951–1954

John Simms
1955–1956

Edwin Mechem
1957–1958

John Burroughs
1959–1960

Edwin Mechem
1961–1962

Tom Bolack
1962

Jack Campbell
1963–1966

David Cargo
1967–1970

Bruce King
1971–1974

Jerry Apodaca
1975–1978

Bruce King
1979–1982

Toney Anaya
1983–1986

Garrey Carruthers
1987–1990

Bruce King
1991–1994

Gary Johnson
1995–2002

Bill Richardson
2003–present

Famous New Mexicans

Edward Abbey, author, Albuquerque

Rudolfo Anaya, author, Pastura

Kathy Baker, actress, Albuquerque

Patrociño Barela, woodcarver, Taos

Joe Bauman, athlete, Roswell

María Benítez, flamenco dancer, Santa Fe

Judy Blume, author, Santa Fe

Ralph Bunche, diplomat, Albuquerque

Ezequiel Cabeza de Baca, politician, Las Vegas

Cathy Carr, swimmer, Albuquerque

Willa Cather, author, Santa Fe

Dennis Chavez, politician, Los Chavez

Ann Nolan Clark, author, Las Vegas

Edward Condon, physicist, Alamogordo

Roy Cooper, rodeo champion, Hobbs

John Denver, singer, Roswell

Bo Diddley, singer, Los Lunas

Pete Domenici, politician, Albuquerque

Erna Fergusson, journalist, author, Albuquerque

Greer Garson, actress, Santa Fe

Robert Goddard, scientist, Roswell

Glenna Goodacre, sculptor, Santa Fe

R.C. Gorman, artist, Taos

Sidney Gutierrez, astronaut, Albuquerque

Donald Hamilton, author, Santa Fe

William Hanna, cartoonist, Melrose

Neil Patrick Harris, actor, Ruidoso

Carl Hatch, politician, Clovis

Tony Hillerman, author, Albuquerque

Conrad Hilton, entrepreneur, San Antonio

Dolores Huerta, labor organizer, Dawson

Peter Hurd, artist, Roswell

Charmayne James, rodeo champion, Clayton

Preston Jones, playwright, actor, Albuquerque

Octaviano Larrazolo, politician, Las Vegas

John Lewis, musician, Albuquerque

Ottmar Liebert, composer, guitarist, Santa Fe

Nancy Lopez, athlete, Roswell

Georgia Lee Witt Lusk, educator, politician, Carlsbad

Gen. Douglas MacArthur, military leader, Ft. Selden

Maria and Julian Martinez, potters, San Ildefonso Pueblo

William "Bill" Mauldin, cartoonist, Santa Fe

Edgar Michell, astronaut, Artesia

N. Scott Momaday, poet, author, Jemez Pueblo

Joseph Montoya, politician, Peña Blanca

Michael Martin Murphey, singer, Red River

John Nichols, author, Taos

Georgia O'Keeffe, artist, Santa Fe

J. Robert Oppenheimer, scientist, Los Alamos

Simon Ortiz, poet, McCartys

Gen. John Pershing, military leader, Fort Bayard

Popé, Pueblo leader, San Juan Pueblo

Ernie Pyle, journalist, Albuquerque

Bill Richardson, diplomat, U.S. ambassador, politician, Santa Fe

Harrison Schmitt, astronaut, politician, Santa Rita

Ernest Thompson Seton, author, naturalist, Santa Fe

Leslie Marmon Silko, author, Laguna Pueblo

Kim Stanley, actress, Tularosa

Roger Staubach, athlete, Roswell

Slim Summerville, actor, Albuquerque

Luci Tapahonso, poet, Shiprock

Clyde Tombaugh, astronomer, Las Cruces

Al Unser, Sr., auto racer, Albuquerque

Bobby Unser, auto racer, Albuquerque

Judith Van Gieson, author, Albuquerque

Pablita Velarde, painter, Santa Clara Pueblo

Lew Wallace, author, Santa Fe

Linda Wertheimer, news commentator, Carlsbad

Richard Wetherill, archaeologist, Chaco Canyon

Gazetteer

This gazetteer is a geographic dictionary that will help you locate and pronounce places in this book. It also gives the latitude and longitude for many places. The page numbers tell you where each place appears on a map (m.) or in the text (t.).

A

Alamogordo (aʹ lə mə gȯrʹ dō) One of the state's driest places; it receives less than 11 inches of precipitation yearly. 32°N; 105°W. (m. 14, t. 20)

Albuquerque (alʹ bə kėrʹ kē) The state's largest city, located in central New Mexico. It is home to the University of New Mexico and many businesses and industries. 35°N; 106°W. (m. 7, t. 20)

B

Basin and Range region (bāʹ sn and rānjʹ rēʹ jən) New Mexico's largest region that extends through the center and into the southwestern corner of the state. (m. 7, t. 7)

Bosque Redondo (bōsʹ kā rā dōnʹ dō) An early Native American reservation. (m. 74, t. 79)

C

El Camino Real (el cäm ēnʹ ō rā älʹ) (The Royal Road) An early road that connected settlements in New Mexico from the south to the north. Traders and settlers followed this route along the Rio Grande north to Santa Fe and Taos. (m. 62, t. 65)

Canadian River (kə nāʹ dē ən rivʹ ər) A major river that flows from the Sangre de Cristo Mountains into the northern part of the Great Plains region and then turns east into Texas. (m. 7, t. 8)

Capulin Mountain (kaʹ pyü lin mounʹ tən) A high point in the Great Plains region; it rises more than 1,200 feet. 36°N; 103°W. (m. 8, t. 8)

Carlsbad Caverns National Park (kärlzʹ bad kavʹ ərnz nashʹ ə nəl pärk) This national park in southeastern New Mexico contains one of the largest caves in the world. Hundreds of thousands of bats live in the caverns and fly out each evening to feed. 32°N; 104°W. (t. 9)

Chaco Culture National Historical Park (chäʹ cō kulʹ chər nashʹ ə nəl hi stôrʹ ə kəl pärk) A historic site near Farmington where archaeologists have learned about ancient people. This area was once home to the Anasazi, who lived in cliff houses. 36°N; 108°W. (m. 48, t. 47)

Chama River Canyon (chäʹ mä rivʹ ər kanʹ yən) The valley of the Chama River in north central New Mexico. It is part of a wilderness area where people enjoy many outdoor activies. (m. 130, t. 134)

Cloudcroft (kloudʹ krȯft) A town in the Sacramento Mountains near the Lincoln National Forest. It is one of the wettest areas in New Mexico. Each year this town receives almost 26 inches of precipitation. 33°N; 105°N. (m. 20, t. 20)

Clovis (klōʹ vis) Location where the remains of early humans were discovered many years ago. 34°N; 103°N. (m. 7, t. 43)

Cochiti Lake (kōʹ chi tē lāk) A village on the Rio Grande in north central New Mexico west of Santa Fe. (m. 96, t. 102)

Colorado Plateau region (kolʹ ə radʹ ō pla tōʹ rēʹ jən) This region covers much of the western part of the state. It features canyons, mesas, mountain ranges, and rocky plateaus. (m. 7, t. 7)

Columbus (kə ləmʹ bəs) A town located in southern New Mexico. In 1916 Pancho Villa, the Mexican revolutionary, crossed the border and raided the town. 31°N; 107°W. (m. 124, t. 84)

Continental Divide (konʹ tə nenʹ tl də vidʹ) A ridge in the Rocky Mountains that divides streams flowing toward the Pacific Ocean from those flowing toward the Atlantic Ocean. (m. 7, t. 12)

E

Eddy County (eʹ dē kounʹ tē) Southeast county where oil and natural gas are located. 32°N; 104°N. (m. 30, t. 35)

F

Farmington (färʹ ming tən) Major mining city. 36°N; 108°W. (m. 7, t. 43)

Fort Sumner (fôrt səmʹ nər) Location of the New Mexico Wind Energy Center. 34°N; 104°W. (m. 116, t. 121)

G

Gila National Forest (hē′ lə nash′ ə nəl fôr′ ist) A national forest in southwestern New Mexico. (m. 18, t. 26)

Glorieta Pass (glō rē et′ əh pas) Union troops won a key battle here, where they drove Confederate forces out of the New Mexico Territory. 35°N; 105°W. (m. 78, t. 78)

Grants (grants) In 1950 a Diné shepherd named Paddy Martinez discovered uranium near Grants in the Colorado Plateau. 35°N; 107°W. (m. 30, t. 35)

Great Plains region (grāt plānz rē′ jən) The region that covers the eastern one-third of New Mexico. The land supports farming, ranching, and mining. (m. 7, t. 7)

K

Kiowa National Grasslands (kī′ ə wə nash′ ə nəl gras′ landz′) A region of high, rolling prairie located in Harding County between the Canadian and Ute Rivers. (t. 8)

L

Las Cruces (läs krü′ sis) A key agricultural center in New Mexico. New Mexico State University is located here. It is well known for agricultural research. White Sands Missile Range is located nearby. 32°N; 106°W. (m. 7, t. 43)

Lea County (lē′ koun′ tē) Oil and natural gas deposits are located in this southeastern county. 32°N; 103°W. (m. 30, t. 35)

Llano Estacado (ya′ nō es′ tə kä′ dō) A high, flat plain south of the Colorado River that has few natural features such as trees or mountains. (t. 9)

Los Alamos (lōs al′ ə mōs) A city in northern New Mexico where scientists during World War II developed an atomic bomb. Today laboratories at Los Alamos continue to conduct research in nuclear energy. 36°N; 106°W. (m. 82, t. 89)

P

Pecos River (pā′ kəs riv′ ər) A major river in the eastern part of the state that flows from the Rocky Mountains region southward into Texas. (m. 7, t. 8)

Philippines (fil′ ə pēnz′) Country that buys more New Mexico products than Canada and New Mexico combined. (t. 127)

R

Raton (rə tōn′) Location where only a few working coal mines remain. 36°N; 104°W. (m. 20, t. 34)

Rio Chama (rē′ ō chä′ mä) A river that has helped shape the land and provides recreation for New Mexicans and visitors. The Rio Chama's canyon is not as long as the Rio Grande Gorge, but it runs even deeper. (m. 11, t. 11)

Rio Grande (rē′ ō grand′) New Mexico's longest river, which flows from north to south through the central part of the state. People have settled along this river for many years. (m. 7, t. 10)

Rio Grande valley (rē′ ō grand′ val′ ē) River valley of Rio Grande. Albuquerque and Las Cruces are located in this valley. (t. 23)

Rocky Mountains region (rok′ ē moun′ tənz rē′ jən) The smallest of New Mexico's four regions, extending south from the Colorado border and ending near Santa Fe. (m. 7, t. 7)

S

San Francisco Mountains (san frən sis′ kō moun′ tənz) A mountain range near the state's western border. (t. 13)

Sangre de Cristo Mountains (sang′ grē də kris′ tō moun′ tənz) This mountain range lies east of Santa Fe. (m. 7, t. 10)

San Juan (san wän′) Spanish settlement in the sixteenth century; located in a fertile valley where the Chama River flows into the Rio Grande. 36°N; 106°W. (m. 59, t. 58)

San Juan River (san wän′ riv′ ər) Major river that crosses the state's northwest corner. (m. 7, t. 12)

Pronunciation Key

a in hat	ō in open	sh in she
ā in age	ȯ in all	th in thin
â in care	ô in order	ᴛʜ in then
ä in far	oi in oil	zh in measure
e in let	ou in out	ə = a in about
ē in equal	u in cup	ə = e in taken
ėr in term	u̇ in put	ə = i in pencil
i in it	ü in rule	ə = o in lemon
ī in ice	ch in child	ə = u in circus
o in hot	ng in long	

Santa Fe (san′ tə fā′) The capital of New Mexico and the oldest capital city in the United States. 35°N; 106°W. (m. 7, t. 43)

Santa Fe Trail (san′ tə fā′ trāl) The major trade route from Missouri to New Mexico. (m. 62, t. 68)

Socorro (sə kôr′ ō) City on the Plains of San Agustin. The Very Large Array, one of the largest radio telescopes in the world, is located west of Socorro. 34°N; 106°W. (m. 59, t. 131)

Taos (tous′) City located in northern New Mexico. 36°N; 105°W. (m. 11, t. 56)

Trinity Site (trin′ ə tē sit) An area near Alamogordo where the United States military tested the world's first atomic bomb. 33°N; 106°W. (m. 82, t. 89)

Valverde (val′ vər dē) Civil War battle fought in New Mexico Territory; near Fort Craig in the southern part of the territory. Confederate troops defeated Union forces. 33°N; 106°W. (m. 78, t. 78)

Wheeler Peak (wē′ lər pēk′) New Mexico's highest point. It is located north of Taos. 36°N; 105°W. (m. 7, t. 10)

Biographical Dictionary

This biographical dictionary tells you about people in this book and how to pronounce their names. The page number tells you where the person first appears in the text.

Armijo, Manuel (mä′ nwel är mē′ hō) (1793?–1853) Mexican who became governor of New Mexico after Albino Pérez. (p. 68)

Becknell, William (bek′ nəl) (1788–1865) A Missouri trader who arrived in Santa Fe in the early 1820s. He was one of the first traders to travel on the Santa Fe Trail. (p. 68)

Boyer, Francis (boi′ ər) (1871–1949) An African American from Georgia who led African American settlers to the New Mexico Territory in the late 1890s. He and his wife Ella founded the town of Blackdom near Roswell. (p. 79)

Bunche, Ralph (bunch) (1903–1971) A diplomat who served in the United Nations. He was the first African American to be awarded a Nobel Prize. (p. 125)

Cabeza de Vaca, Alvar Núñez (äl vär nü′ nyez kä bē′ zu dā vä kä) (1490?–1560?) A Spanish explorer who may have been one of the first Europeans to see what is now New Mexico in 1536. (p. 55)

Chacon, Soledad (sō le däd′ chä kōn′) (1890–1936) One of the first two women in New Mexico to be elected to a statewide office. (p. 85)

Chavez, Dennis (chä′ vez) (1888–1962) A U.S. Senator who worked to protect the rights of all New Mexicans. A statue of Chavez stands in the United States Capitol in Washington, D.C. (p. 87)

Coronado, Francisco Vásquez de (frän sēs′ kō väs′ kez dā kôr ə nä′ dō) (1510–1554) Spanish explorer who led an expedition into present-day New Mexico. (p. 56)

Eckles, Isabel (ek′ ulz) (1877–1971) One of the first two women in New Mexico to be elected to a statewide office. (p. 85)

Espejo, Antonio de (ant ō′ nyō dā ā spā′ hō) (? –1585) Spanish explorer who led an expedition into present-day New Mexico. He was the first explorer to call the area "New Mexico." (p. 57)

Estevan (es tā′ bän) (1500?–1539) An enslaved African who participated in early expeditions in present-day New Mexico. (p. 55)

Gadsden, James (gadz′ dən) (1788–1858) United States representative to Mexico. He arranged for the United States to buy land from Mexico. (p. 75)

L

Lawrence, D.H. (lawr′ uhns) (1885–1930) A British writer who lived in Taos for a while during the 1920s. (p. 86)

M

Magoffin, Susan Shelby (mä gof′ in) (1827–1855) One of the first American women to travel the Santa Fe Trail. She wrote a journal during the journey. (p. 68)

Martinez, Maria (mär tē′ nez) (1880s?–1980) A potter from San Ildefonso pueblo who created a unique type of pottery. (p. 86)

Martinez, Paddy (mär tē′ nez) (1881–1969) A Diné shepherd who discovered uranium near Grants in 1950. (p. 35)

McDonald, William C. (mək don′ əld) (1858–1918) A rancher from Carrizozo who was elected New Mexico's first state governor. (p. 83)

N

Niza, Friar Marcos de (mär′ kōs dā ne′ sä) (1495–1558) A Spanish missionary who explored present-day New Mexico in 1539. (p. 56)

O

O'Keeffe, Georgia (ō kēf′) (1887–1986) A well-known painter who lived near Abiquiu. Much of her art reflects the New Mexico landscape. (p. 11)

Oñate, Don Juan de (don′ hwȯn′ dā ō nyä′ tā) (1550?–1626) He was appointed governor of New Mexico and established the first permanent Spanish settlement. (p. 58)

Otero-Warren, Adelina "Nina" (ä dē lē′ nə ō târ′ ō wôr′ en) (1881–1951) A women who served in government positions related to education and Native American services from 1917 to 1929. (p. 85)

P

Pérez, Albino (äl bē′ nō pâr′ ez) (? –1837) Mexican governor of New Mexico who tried to increase taxes. Settlers rebelled against him in 1837. (p. 68)

Pershing, John (pėr′ shing) (1860–1948) United States Army general who led United States forces searching for Pancho Villa. During World War I, Pershing commanded United States forces in Europe. (p. 84)

Pike, Zebulon (pīk) (1779–1813) An explorer who led an expedition from the United States, which entered New Mexico in 1807. (p. 67)

Popé (pō pā′) (1630?–1690?) A Pueblo leader who organized the Pueblo Revolt against the Spanish in 1680. A statue of Popé has been commissioned for placement in the U.S. Capitol building in Washington, D.C. (p. 60)

R

Richardson, Bill (ri′ chard sən) (1947–) A New Mexican elected governor in 2002. He previously represented the United States at the United Nations. (p. 125)

S

Silko, Leslie Marmon (sil′ kō) (1948–) A Native American writer of novels and poems about Native American culture, history, myths, and traditions. (p. 133)

V

Vargas, Don Diego de (don dē ā′ gō dā vär′ gəs) (? –1704) A Spanish soldier who regained control of New Mexico following the Pueblo Revolt. (p. 63)

Villa, Pancho (pän′ chō vē′ yə) (1877–1923) Mexican revolutionary who led a raid against the town of Columbus, New Mexico, in 1916. (p. 84)

W

White, Jim (wīt) (1882–1946) New Mexico cowhand who explored Carlsbad Caverns in the early 1900s. (p. 9)

Pronunciation Key

a in hat	ō in open	sh in she
ā in age	ȯ in all	th in thin
â in care	ô in order	ᴛʜ in then
ä in far	oi in oil	zh in measure
e in let	ou in out	ə = a in about
ē in equal	u in cup	ə = e in taken
ėr in term	u̇ in put	ə = i in pencil
i in it	ü in rule	ə = o in lemon
ī in ice	ch in child	ə = u in circus
o in hot	ng in long	

Glossary

This glossary will help you understand and pronounce the terms and vocabulary words in this book. The page number tells you where the word first appears.

 **A**

acequia (ä sā′ kē ə) A community ditch system that distributes water. (p. 33)

ally (al′ ī) A person, group, or nation united with another for some special purpose. (p. 84)

aquifer (ăk′ wi fėr) A wide layer of underground earth or rock that contains water. (p. 32)

archaeologist (är kē äl′ u jist) A person who studies buildings, tools, pottery, weapons, and other objects from the past to learn about people who lived long ago. (p. 47)

architecture (är kə tek′ chər) The style or special manner of building. (p. 42)

artifact (är′ tə fakt) An object that was made and used a long time ago. (p. 47)

 **B**

basin (bā′ sn) A bowl-shaped area of land surrounded by higher land. (p. 12)

bill (bil) A proposed law. (p. 109)

bond (bond) A certificate that promises to pay back the buyer over time the amount paid plus interest. (p. 107)

budget (buj′ it) A plan for using money. (p. 125)

 **C**

checking account (chek′ ing ə kount′) A bank account from which checks can be written to pay for products and services. (p. 117)

cinder cone (sin′ dər cōn) A type of volcano made of loose material such as volcanic rocks and ash. (p. 8)

citizenship (sit′ ə zən ship) The rights and responsibilities of being a citizen. (p. 102)

community college (kə myü′ nə tē kol′ ij) A school that offers the first two years of college courses. (p. 97)

crater (krā′ tər) The bowl-shaped hole around the opening of a volcano. (p. 8)

 **D**

deposit (di poz′ it) Money put in a certain place, such as a bank, for safekeeping. (p. 117)

district (dis′ trikt) A part of a state or city marked off for a special purpose. (p. 109)

dry farming (drī′ fär′ ming) A method of farming that uses only rainwater to grow crops. (p. 36)

 **E**

ecosystem (ē′ kō sis′ təm) A physical environment with its community of living things. (p. 24)

environment (en vī′ rən mənt) All the surrounding conditions and influences that affect the growth of living things. (p. 22)

expedition (ek′ spə dish′ ən) A long and carefully organized trip, usually made for a particular purpose. (p. 55)

 G

groundwater (ground′ wȯ′ tər) Water that flows or seeps downward, soaks the rock below the soil, and supplies springs and wells. (p. 32)

 **H**

hemisphere (hem′ ə sfir) Half of Earth's surface. (p. 19)

high-tech industry (hī′ tek′ in′ də strē) An industry that uses the latest form of technology to make new goods and services. (p. 119)

historian (hi stôr′ ē ən) A person who writes about history. (p. 47)

homesteader (hōm′ sted′ ər) A settler granted land by the United States government. (p. 77)

hunter-gatherer (hun′ tər gaтн′ ər ər) A person who hunts animals and gathers wild plants for food. (p. 48)

 **I**

interest (in′ tər ist) Money paid for the use of someone else's money. (p. 107)

L

land grant (land′ grant) A gift of land. (p. 64)

land use (land′ yüs) What should be done with a piece of land. (p. 122)

M

majority (mə jôr′ ə tē) The larger number, or more than half. (p. 109)

majority rule (mə jôr′ ə tē rül) Decisions are made according to what most people want. (p. 109)

market (mär′ kit) A country or area in which a company sells its goods. (p. 126)

mesa (mā′ sə) A small, high plateau with steep sides and a flat top. (p. 8)

migrate (mi′ grāt) To move from one place in order to settle in another. (p. 58)

minority (mə nôr′ ə tē) A group within a country or state that differs in race or religion from the larger part of the population. (p. 114)

N

NAFTA (naf′ tə) The North American Free Trade Agreement, designed to encourage trade between the United States and its two closest neighbors. (p. 126)

natural gas (nach′ ər əl gas) A gas that forms underground. (p. 9)

nomad (nō′ mad) Someone who moves from place to place to find food and other needed items. (p. 48)

O

observatory (ab zèr′ və tôr′ ē) A building with equipment for watching and studying objects in space. (p. 131)

P

port of entry (port′ ov en′ tree) An official place where travelers or goods enter or leave a country. (p. 126)

predator (pred′ ə tər) An animal that lives by killing and eating other animals. (p. 26)

public good (pub′ lik gůd) The good of all the people. (p. 114)

R

reservoir (rez′ ər vwär) A place where water is stored for use. (p. 31)

resident (rez′ ə dənt) A person living in a place. (p. 97)

responsibility (ri spon′ sə bil′ ə tē) Something that you have a duty to do. (p. 101)

revolve (ri volv′) To move in a circle around a point. (p. 19)

right (rīt) Something to which you have a claim, or something you deserve. (p. 100)

rotate (rō′ tāt) To spin on an axis. (p. 19)

S

savings account (sā′ vingz ə kount′) An account that pays interest. (p. 117)

suburb (sub′ èrb′) A type of community located near a large city. (p. 43)

supercomputer (sü′ pər kəm pyü′ tər) A very powerful, high-speed computer. (p. 131)

surface water (sèr′ fis wȯ′ tər) Water on Earth's surface in reservoirs, rivers, and lakes. (p. 32)

T

tariff (tar′ if) A kind of tax that is added to the cost of imported goods. (p. 127)

territory (ter′ ə tôr′ ē) An area that is not admitted as a state but has its own lawmaking group. (p. 70)

tributary (trib′ yə ter′ ē) A stream or river that flows into a larger river. (p. 13)

turquoise (tèr′ koiz) A sky-blue or greenish-blue mineral often used as a gem. (p. 34)

Pronunciation Key

a in hat	ō in open	sh in she
ā in age	ȯ in all	th in thin
â in care	ô in order	ᴛʜ in then
ä in far	oi in oil	zh in measure
e in let	ou in out	ə = a in about
ē in equal	u in cup	ə = e in taken
ėr in term	ů in put	ə = i in pencil
i in it	ü in rule	ə = o in lemon
ī in ice	ch in child	ə = u in circus
o in hot	ng in long	

Index

This index lists the page numbers on which topics appear in this book. Page numbers after an *m* refer to maps. Page numbers after a *c* refer to charts and graphs. Page numbers after a *p* refer to photographs.

Credits

Every effort has been made to secure permission and provide appropriate credit for photographic material. The publisher deeply regrets any omission and pledges to correct errors called to its attention in subsequent editions.

Unless otherwise acknowledged, all photographs are the property of Scott Foresman, a division of Pearson Education.

Photo locators denoted as follows: Top (T), Center (C), Bottom (B), Left (L), Right (R), Background (Bkgd)

Text
From *Down the Santa Fe Trail and Into Mexico: The Diary of Susan Shelby Magoffin.* New Haven, CT: Yale University Press.
From *Storyteller* by Leslie Marmon Silko. Copyright (c) 1981 by Leslie Marmon Silko. All Rights Reserved.

Fair Use
From the Silver City Daily Press, Jan. 4, 2000 (letter to the editor, 1_sentences) as it appears in the Autumn 99-vol. 3 no. 4 Newsletter for the Upper Gila Watershed Alliance.
Quote by Caren Cowan as it appears in the Citizen Review Online, September 2000.
Quote from *María: The Potter of San Ildefonso* by Alice Marriott.
From *Phoenix: The Posthumous Papers of D. H. Lawrence* edited by Edward D. McDonald.
From *Coronado, Knight of Pueblos and Plains* by Herbert E. Bolton.
From *International Conference of the Institute of Pacific Relations,* December 1942.
From "Jim White's Own Story: The Discovery and History of Carlsbad Caverns"; James Larkin White as told to Frank Ernest Nicholson.
Quote from *Southwesterners Write* by T. M. Pearce and A. P. Thomason.
Quote from *New Mexico Rio Grande and Other Essays,* by Tony Hillerman.
From *The Legacy of Maria Poveka Martinez:* by Richard L. Spivey.
From http://senate.gov.
Quote by Francisco Vasquez de Coronado.
Song "O', Fair New Mexico" by Elizabeth Garrett, adopted in 1917.

Maps
MapQuest.com

Illustrations
19   Greg Harris
46   Kathlyn Shadle
61   Joel Iskowitz
62, 126 Lee Woolery
69   Dan Krovatin
135   Bill Fox

Photographs

Cover
(C) © David Muench/Corbis
(BR) © George H. H. Huey/Corbis
(Bkgd) © Comstock Inc.

Front Matter
iii   (T) © John Sloan/O'Connor/The Anschutz Collection

Chapter 1
1   (C) © John Sloan/O'Connor/The Anschutz Collection
2   (B) © Jeremy Woodhouse/Masterfile Corporation
3   (CL) Corbis, (TR) © Donald M. Jones/DRK Photo, (C,TL) Corbis, (CR) © Danny Lehman/Corbis
6   (BL) © Craig Aurness/Corbis
9   (B) © Tom Bean/DRK Photo, (TR) Santa Fe System Lines/Library of Congress
10   (T) © Liz Hymans/Corbis
11   (TR) © Buddy Mays/Corbis
12   (T) © Kevin Fleming/Corbis
13   (B) © George H. H. Huey/Corbis
14   (B) © Catherine Karnow/Woodfin Camp & Associates, (TR) © Darrell Gulin/Corbis
15   (T) © Adam Woolfitt/Woodfin Camp & Associates
16   (BL) Wiley/Wales, (BR) © David Muench/Corbis, (C) © Jim Sugar/Corbis
17   (Bkgd) National Geographic/Getty Images, (CL) Santa Fe System Lines/Library of Congress
18   (BL) © Gary R. Zahm/DRK Photo
20   (C) © Joel Bennett/Peter Arnold, Inc.
21   (T) © Buddy Mays/Travel Stock
22   (T) © Richard A. Cooke/Corbis
23   (BR) © David Muench/Corbis

Credits